Before You Say Anything

First published in the United States by St. Martin's Press, an imprint of St. Martin's Publishing Group

www.stmartins.com

Designed by Jonathan Bennett

The Library of Congress Cataloging-in-Publication Data
is available upon request.

ISBN 978-1-250-27402-1 (hardcover)

ISBN 978-1-250-27403-8 (ebook)

First Edition: April 2022

10 9 8 7 6 5 4 3 2 1

Before You Say Anything

THE UNTOLD STORIES AN
FAILPROOF STRATEGIES O
VERY DISCREET SPEECHWR

Victoria Wellma

ST. MARTIN'S PRESS
NEW YORK

To Louisiana and Camellia, whose natural gift for nonstop speaking is one of the greatest joys of my work as a mother.

And to Nathan—the most determined and loving collaborator I could ever dream of having—for reminding all three of us that listening is just as important.

Contents

Contents

A Gentle Warning

One of the things I love about my eldest child, Louisiana (that's her real name—she'd be livid if I deprived her of the credit), is that she almost never follows the instructions on her building and crafting sets. Boxes and boxes of Legos, origami kits, jewelry crafting, Magna-Tiles, you name it—while they all come with detailed step-by-step directions that promise a perfectly homogenized execution of a spaceship or friendship bracelet, my daughter, Lou Lou, shows no interest at all in making something in the manner expected of her. I admit that when I find myself cleaning up threads and minuscule wheel parts—too tired to goad or bribe her—I often discover the tiny instruction booklet discarded on the floor, and stuff it back in the box hoping that maybe one day she might commit to the episodic process of making a toy or art piece from start to finish. The appeal of this is nothing more than a guaranteed period of quiet and focus, because when she improvises you never know how long she'll keep herself busy. She's the quintessential first child.

But in many ways I greatly admire Lou Lou's tenacity and rebellion. It may just be in her blood—my side of the family is a bunch of stubborn men and women who like to do things their own way. *Who says I can't do it like this??!* My mother has her own method for everything. She even sometimes pronounces words in a way only she can understand. But she also thinks her own way is the only and correct way. *Why would you not do it this way?!* I like to think Lou Lou has found the sweet spot right in the middle. She knows instinctively that striving to follow someone else's template or prescribed method of doing something stifles her own freedom of expression and problem-solving capabilities, but she is equally aware that aspiring to correctness leads to unimaginative and uncreative outcomes with little space for outside voices or authentic connection.

Oh, who am I kidding? She probably just can't be bothered to flip the pages and find the right pieces.

In this book, however, I will manifest this optimistic interpretation of Lou Lou's Lego building strategy. I don't believe that there can exist a step-by-step guide to a pursuit as idiosyncratic, artistic, and human as crafting and delivering an exceptional speech for any occasion. To truly excel in this area is simply not as easy as piecing together a few bricks to make something that someone next door would do the very same way. The mark of a successful speech is one that offers the audience something new. How could there possibly be a how-to? How could there be a step-by-step? There can only be, therefore, a how-*I,* and in this case, while I won't go as far as annointing myself the arbiter of correctness, in sharing my method I will make this promise to you: I will take you on an entertaining journey and leave you in a place where

A Gentle Warning

the next time someone asks you to make a speech, you'll know exactly where to start, what to strive for, and how to get there. And the speech will be a damn sight better than if you hadn't read the book.

Before You Say Anything

Introduction

Of all the talents bestowed upon men, none is so precious as the gift of oratory. He who enjoys it wields a power more durable than that of a great king. He is an independent force in the world. Abandoned by his party, betrayed by his friends, stripped of his offices, whoever can command this power is still formidable.

—WINSTON CHURCHILL

What he said, but the less chauvinistic version.

—VICTORIA WELLMAN

One of my favorite clients, Sherri, an astronaut whose account of going to space makes me cry like a baby every time, once told me that GPS coordinates were one of the few things the world can agree on. I'd say there's another thing: the universal desire not to completely suck when we speak in public.

Feelings range from the kind of deep-seated, clinically diagnosed social anxiety that makes the prospect of standing in front of a roomful of people equivalent to being water-boarded, at one end of the spectrum, to the other end, where exhibitionists actively seek out the spotlight and fantasize about a standing ovation. And then there are the people in between who don't particularly relish the opportunity but would probably choose it over, say, being stung by a bee, because they recognize that getting better at public speaking, while potentially just as uncomfortable, has an outsized payoff.

Whatever negative feelings the prospect of speaking may trigger, you pretty much have two options. One is to try to remedy the fear by addressing the psychological drivers. For this you might consult a coach. Or a pharmacist. The other is to improve the content so that when you step up to the podium or the microphone and the heart palpitations begin to subside, you have something fucking great to say.

Though I usually warn people against starting a speech with the apologetic disclaimer "I'm a bit nervous," I do recall granting this wish to one client, but not because she was making excuses.

> *I'm sure that I'm not the first parent to say this here, but it's really hard to describe how I feel today. Perhaps I can explain it like this: I took a public speaking class back in college, and I dropped out because every time it was my turn to speak, I thought I was gonna die. Right now I feel completely the opposite—my heart isn't failing, it's exploding. I look around the room and all I see are faces of people who know and love my daughter and who have in some way helped her get here today. If I could hand out a stone for all those I need to thank, I'd have to hire a forklift to carry them. And the nearest rental company is seventy-six miles away—I checked it out.*

Introduction

Rebecca was speaking at her daughter's graduation from an equine therapy treatment center. After Izzy turned semi-pro at snowboarding at a very young age, she had fallen in with a bad crowd and started getting in trouble with the police a lot. Coming to terms with the fact that Izzy had a Xanax addiction and was heading down a slippery slope—the kind that couldn't be navigated by a snowboard—Rebecca did what any parent would try to avoid at all costs: she "gooned" her daughter. This, I learned from Rebecca, means that at 4:00 a.m. one night, a guy from a rehab center came to the house and took Izzy away to a wilderness camp for ninety days. Amazingly, after the ninety days, Izzy acknowledged she was in a better emotional space and agreed to attend a ranch school where tending to horses provided a frame-work of accountability, compassion, and other such values that parents struggle to instill in their children. By the time Izzy reached her graduation ceremony, Rebecca was pos-itively champing at the bit to get up onstage and tell her daughter how proud of her she was—and, as was the cus-tom, dedicate a stone to each person she wanted to thank. (I researched the rental companies in the area; the seventy-six miles was no joke.) Rebecca had come to the realization that when you're invested in your message and you see the crowd as allies, not enemies, there is much to relish about sharing that message.

The problem, as poor Izzy can vouch, is that buying Xanax is a lot easier. Just ask Izzy. From writing to delivery, the pro-cess of crafting a brilliant speech for most people promises only a grueling, often unsatisfying, frustrating, and unknow-able gauntlet of questions:

Where do I begin?

How do I put the thoughts together?

How do I make sure I say what they want?

How do I make it funny?

Where do I stand? How do I stand? Should I stand?

Then the panic becomes more specific . . .

Oprah is speaking right before me.

Most of the audience are comedy writers and I'm an accountant.

I've had a genius idea, but it's hard to articulate quantum physics.

If I say the wrong thing, I could spark an international disaster.

Something incredible happened to me, but words don't do it justice.

I used to sleep with the groom.

You may be one of the millions who have panic-scoured the internet. *How to write a great speech,* you desperately typed into Google's search bar, only to come across hackneyed tips written by junior editors at lifestyle magazines. You might have gone to YouTube, where at the very best you might have found a video of a gentle-mannered Chris Anderson in a pair of crisply ironed chinos calmly outlining the TED method, which, despite the charming soundtrack of trills and sprightly dings, and some lovely graphics, only made you more intimidated by the idea that your one amazing "idea" maybe isn't amazing enough. Or maybe you'll have taken your problem to the bookstore, where you found emotionally devoid corporate manuals written by communications experts and fans of Woodrow Wilson.

The problem isn't that all the experts are crap. I don't have that much hubris. It's that there aren't that many actual experts, let alone any who, without knowing a thing about you, can provide the kind of specific advice you need. To this day I've never even met another speechwriter, either at a social gathering or a networking schmooze. It's sort of the occupational equivalent of being born a leap-year baby, on February 29 (as I was—and yet I know four other people with the same birthday). Filmmakers, bankers, swimming instructors, tree doctors, pageant queens, and hackers—from the most obvious to the most niche, I've encountered professionals from every facet of the workforce. I even came across an ex-Mossad locksmith once. I've met authors, copywriters, journalists, feature writers, scriptwriters. Every kind of writer you can imagine—I mean, I live in Brooklyn; everyone in my neighborhood is a writer. But none of them are speechwriters.

Unsurprisingly, when people find out how I make a living, the interrogation begins. The first thing they want to know is whose speeches I've written, hoping I'll spill the beans on a famous politician or celebrity. This makes sense if we're to believe Yuval Noah Harari's theory that *Homo sapiens* conquered the world in large part because of their proclivity for gossip. They clearly didn't have NDAs and discretionary policies back then.

I can't blame them. It's entirely fair to presume that only the wealthy and influential have speechwriters. But this exclusivity is precisely why I started my company, The Oratory Laboratory.

I won't be coy: I'm not cheap. Thomas Edison said genius was 1 percent inspiration and 99 percent sweat. Well, so is speechwriting—there are no shortcuts—and we all know the adage about time and money. The Oratory Laboratory, however, was built on a more ideological and egalitarian belief (I am, after all, a Brit), that everyone deserves a speechwriter and almost as many people need one. It was a way to acknowledge that most people, regardless of class, race, political affiliation, wealth, age, sex, gender, blood group, or zip code, have at one time (or maybe even four) been invited or been given the opportunity to speak about something in a room full of people and that almost as many do a crummy job of it. It didn't seem fair to the speakers or their agonized audiences to ignore their plight.

It used to be presumed that speaking in public required confidence and charisma and was a skill exercised only by the elite and well-educated few—lawyers, politicians, corporate bigwigs, and others in positions of power and privilege—while the mostly disenfranchised masses just watched.

But all that has changed. The technology revolution has raised the stakes for everyone.

Today on YouTube, 9 million viewers can mock the "worst best-man speech ever"—and the same 9 million can model their vision for the future on the viral video of a commencement speech delivered by an era-defining thought leader.

Now we have tweets and blogs and Instagram feeds that amplify our own political manifestos, personal soliloquies, and professional aspirations—with zero filter and every expectation that there is an audience who is listening and cares.

Introduction

We have TED, The Moth, and StoryCorps. And we have conferences, retreats, and blockbuster events like SXSW that have multiplied the number of people with access to the once-exclusive spotlight by an increasingly immeasurable number.

Nowadays, an ability to express yourself in public, thoughtfully and without fear, in an authentic voice, has become both a rite of passage and an essential skill for anyone who wants to make a difference, however modest or grand—whether in their family, in the community, in the workplace, or at the podium in front of thousands. What better way to expand your networks, garner respect, and rise up the totem pole (social or professional) than by successfully captivating an audience with your ideas? And yet the conventional wisdom around what resonates for today's speakers and their audiences has failed to evolve, so speakers are left to wonder how they will craft a speech that provides the individuality, originality, and authenticity our culture demands.

As advertisers and marketers continue to draw on human experiences and authenticity to raise brand awareness and attract clicks, the most human way to connect to an audience has been left behind in terms of innovation. A powerful speech is unlike any other form of communication. It wins elections, creates movements, inspires our peers, and brings people together. It deserves a new way of thinking.

In the early fall of 2008, my then-boyfriend, Nathan, and I found ourselves in a minivan on I-95 bouncing our way south back to New York City from a wedding in New Hampshire. At the time nothing in our profiles indicated we had a future together. He was a comedy and improv nerd from a deteriorating industrial town in Massachusetts. His family was complicated—he had way more parents and stepfamily than I did. He wore square-toed dress shoes, loved Blue Man Group, and talked about his friends using weird names they'd given each other during experimental workshops. In contrast, I grew up in a snobby central London neighborhood in an unhinged but committed family who, until quite recently, generally procreated in twos. I hated square-toed shoes and Blue Man Group, and aside from a tight-knit group of girl-friends, the kinds of people I knew in New York had names that were memorable only when you needed to get into an exclusive bar. Nathan was a tonic to that world, the kind that didn't need vodka. He reacquainted me with my more authentic self—the one who could quote John Hughes movies from start to end and had been happiest dancing around in leg warmers at drama school. We started dating in April, but by midsummer we'd passed an important relationship benchmark by making out to *Purple Rain*—the entire movie, not just the song. It was intense. By early fall, we had passed the ultimate relationship stress test by attending three summer weddings as each other's official date.

On our drive home from the last, the conversation turned to the subject of the wedding speeches and how embarrassingly bad they'd been. I recalled the pained expressions, bemused glances, and awkward silences that had torpedoed the otherwise pleasurable crescendo of eye-catching décor, delicious food, and potent signature cocktails. At each of these weddings the ill-conceived and poorly executed speeches had hijacked the moment—transforming the room from vibrant and boisterous to quiet, uncomfortable, and dull.

At the first wedding, the maid of honor had talked exclusively about herself. She told every story that should have been about the bride as if she were the protagonist in her best friend's life story. "She always got so pissed when I . . . She hated it when I . . . It was so funny when our friend Jenna and I . . ." It was so self-absorbed and self-flattering that she ended up just sounding bitchy. In the second wedding, the best man delivered an A-to-Z character breakdown of the groom. It was so long and so boring the guests had nothing to do but refill their glasses. By the letter *D* we were drunk. By *W* we were wasted. The third and final wedding featured a speech from the father of the bride that amounted to a chronological retelling of his daughter's life, from her first stuffed animal she couldn't live without and the high school sports teams and trophies to the wonderful internship she'd won and the sought-after job she now had. By the time we got to her college days, I'd already fashioned about nineteen original origami sculptures from my napkin, which is hard to do with slippery polyester.

At that moment in the minivan I realized that no one should ever have to sit in silence and be subjected to an hour of generic, clichéd, sentimental drivel again, nor should anyone ever have to experience the guilt of committing such a crime. "Someone needs to help these people!" I blurted out. "Someone must save the world from bad speeches!"

Now, I didn't go to Georgetown and study political science or intern on a political campaign. I never wrote speeches for my boss. In fact, while my sister devoured books (quite literally—she tore off and chewed the corners of the pages), I barely even read as a child. When George H. W. Bush was delivering Peggy Noonan's famous "Read my lips—no new taxes" line, I was in middle school and busy polishing a series of speeches of my own that reflected on the most crucial topics of the day, including great white sharks, snowboarding, and, most fittingly, the history of Alcoholics Anonymous. Yet despite my enjoyment of this type of assignment, I didn't take writing seriously as an adult until I enrolled at drama school in London and realized that Shakespeare really was as good as everyone insisted. Shortly after graduating and moving to New York to pursue the American dream of waiting in line at Equity auditions, I found there was plenty of time between line runs to ruminate on all my brilliant ideas for TV shows and memoirs. I don't know how many writers can put a date on the day they began to write, but I honestly can. It was January 14, 2008. I wrote a cocky letter to a former opinion writer and satirical genius at *The Times* in London in response to an article about English expats in New York. And I'll never forget my sister's response when I sent her a copy, feeling very pleased with my debut effort. She wrote back: "That's brilliant! Maybe you should be a journalist! You could have a column about the 'Englishwoman in New York.' You've got a real talent. Xxxxx." That was all I needed—an endorsement from my closest ally. I wrote essays about being an English girl in New York, a pilot episode about being an English girl in New York, and a one-woman stage show about being an English girl in New York. The casting directors of *Law and Order* weren't quite as interested in a spontaneous recital of my own work as I'd hoped, but the well-established and influential writers at the arts club where I worked were more generous with their time and attention and were even encouraging with their feedback. To hell with all those casting directors who didn't want me in their movies and the waiting rooms full of girls who looked like me with better hair and makeup. Dick Wolf could s*** it.

While continuing to polish my autobiographical magnum opera, I built up my resume as a feature writer, reporter, copywriter, producer, and voice-over artist, contributing articles and scripts to newsrooms and networks, and by the time the lightbulb went off in that minivan on I-95 I had zero experience speechwriting beyond a couple of wedding hits, but I knew I possessed every tool the job required. That day Nathan and I committed to the challenge of saving the world from bad speeches. And then, just like Joe Scarborough and Mika Brzezinski—whose *Morning Joe* promo I scripted years before they went public as a couple, only to be told that the way it highlighted their chemistry was too suggestive—Nathan and I committed to each other. Joe and Mika were right: it made things much easier. (I still have a cut of the promo, by the way.)

Ten years later, I've crafted more than five hundred speeches for almost as many people, and I can quite honestly say I've had just as much if not more fun writing their stories. The most rewarding collaborations and exciting alliances have not been with celebrities who are tirelessly corralled and controlled by publicists or managers and seldom digress from talking points that have been nipped and tucked in "personal branding" sessions. The best experiences have been with the hundreds of other speakers—the counterterrorism cyber experts, creators of TV shows, art buyers, Supreme Court justices, and regular people—who, in simply trying to articulate how they feel about people they love and issues they care about, not only take me on a path of incredible learning but discover for themselves the import of their stories and what it is to feel heard. If there is one thing that I cannot get enough of, it is hearing how transformed the speaker has been by the process of reaching deep within in order to externalize the feelings they might not have shared, the hunches they've been too nervous to voice, the ideas that without oxygen hadn't yet crystallized.

I don't know if I've written as many speeches as Cody Keenan or Jon Favreau (both of whom wrote speeches for Barack Obama), but I am certain that I've written for many more people. So sure in fact that a few years ago I tasked an intern with researching the *Guinness Book of World Records* application process. I've always thought that would be such a great line to tout: "world record holding speechwriter!" Shame the paperwork was too much of a bore. Having written for so many people, however, I've been forced to scrutinize, iterate on, and codify a process that is flexible enough to work with each and every one of those people and on each and every speech. It's a creative strategy that respects the fact that every person and every speech is unique, and therefore every structure, every subtext, every joke, every setup, and every conclusion must be unique too. That a protest speech does not consist of the same elements as a commencement address. That a rally speech isn't a client presentation, an award speech isn't a fundraiser, and a keynote isn't a company roast. It's not about the specific building blocks (or Lego pieces, if you will); rather, it's about gathering the best raw materials and imagining a speech so original that only you could have written it.

"How do you do it, then?" is the next thing people want to know when I'm done with the impassioned manifesto. Interested and skeptical parties alike can't quite fathom how this process would maintain integrity and authenticity. How do

I capture a speaker's personality and their ideas? And the answer I give them is that I too ask questions. Lots of questions. Silly questions, inappropriate questions, irrelevant questions, disturbing questions, provocative questions, and searching questions.

By invitation, I put on the speaker's shoes and walk around in their world, exploring their perspectives and their ideas as best I can. And then I put my shoes back on to interrogate those ideas and perspectives, recast them, and articulate them in a way that captures the imagination of the people listening. I ask myself questions about what I don't know I don't know. I ask myself questions I think the audience would want to know. I go down internet rabbit holes, unearth question marks around every corner, interrogate everything I hear and read in the media that might pertain to the speech, and wrestle with structures and frameworks and central themes. I ask questions right up until the last period on the first draft, knowing that if I start from a place of ignorance and am willing to put in the work, this curiosity, open-mindedness, and fearlessness will take me where I need to go. It is a grueling but blissful process.

As a speaker, your own shoes are familiar and comfortable. You know your subject. You know your experience. You're close to it. But wearing your own shoes will always limit how far you can go in writing a speech, and—like a worn-in, worn-down pair of slippers—may even cause you to stumble. As you begin to think about how to package and share your thoughts and ideas, you will always do best to suppose you know nothing about your speech at the outset and commit to treading this long, circuitous journey of revelation. The danger of not doing so and anticipating your success prematurely is that you trip up when it's too late to recover.

I can't promise that this book will magically turn you into a brilliant wordsmith. What I can do is show you how to notice things that I notice—the observations that motivate my hundreds of questions, the subsequent investigations of which turn a mediocre narrative into a smart, gutsy, and emotionally resonant address.

You don't have to be a literary mastermind or to have climbed a mountain (and onto a TED stage) to be a brilliant speaker. As Chef Gusteau says in that grade-school cult classic *Ratatouille,* "Anybody can cook." It doesn't mean everyone will be able to use truffles like Thomas Keller. But it acknowledges that everyone can make something that leaves their guests wanting more.

First, you have to know how to ask the right questions.

Here's mine. Are you ready?

À l'attaque!

PART ONE
The Brief

1

(Great) Expectations and Intentions

Deciding What Kind of Speech You're Going to Make

Where *the hell do I begin?* It's a common dilemma for anyone faced with the momentous and intimidating task of sorting through anything jumbled—be it the kitchen junk drawer, your dead grandma's house, or that secret storage unit filled with embarrassing mementos from the time you were in an improv troupe (that little storage space you worked so hard to keep hidden from your new girlfriend but whose $100 monthly fee has become problematic now that she's your wife). And there's nothing more psychologically defeating than when that jumble is a nebulous and intangible collection of thoughts, ideas, and memories that you can't pick up one by one, label with a Sharpie, and shove in a pile somewhere.

I'm not going to lie—writing a speech is a messy affair. You have to roll up your sleeves and commit to a few days, consecutive or otherwise, submerged in chaos and unanswered questions. But the good news is that by the time you get around to crafting language around those early turbulent ruminations in your head, you'll already have figured out exactly where to put them and how to label them, and you'll have thrown out the garbage you don't need. And while the steps you might take are far from orderly or sequential, the process of writing a speech is just as intentional and strategic as cleaning out any hoarder's house, every bit as satisfying, and far less likely to reveal a commune of rabid stray cats living in the bathroom vanity.

This wasn't unfortunately the case for Carly, who had a litter of metaphorical stray cats in her metaphorical bathroom. I will say, it's not every day that I'm asked to help craft an autobiographical eulogy from beyond the grave for a person who is alive and kicking and will be for the foreseeable future. But this is what Carly wanted, and her list of specifics was long, including the expectation that the eulogy would be delivered at the funeral by her daughter. The funeral, she explained (and hoped), wouldn't be for another thirty years. She was still young and, as far as she knew, in good health. But she was determined that, once she was in the ground, she would finally get to air out her grievances. She wanted everyone to know exactly how overwhelmingly they had failed her. How her father had been the only one in a large family who made her feel loved. How alone and isolated she felt, even with five siblings, after he had passed away. She wanted it to be a "hey, you pretty much ruined my life and I don't forgive you" farewell, but seemed to think we could balance that with humor and celebration. I thought about Hunter S. Thompson's funeral, where his ashes were shot into the sky from a cannon while "Spirit in the Sky" played in the background, and wondered if maybe we could set Carly's big showdown to a peppy soundtrack. "I Will Survive"? No, that wouldn't work, since she'd be dead. I was going to need her Spotify playlist, so I added that to the long list of questions I had for her. Others included: Did her daughter know she'd been tapped for the "Hey, I kind of despise you all" speech, or did she want this privileged role to be a surprise? Might she consider another option, like gathering the immediate family around a meal and making a statement (that we could help her write) sooner than, say, death? Had she thought about whether in twenty to thirty years she might feel differently? Would her message conflict with the other celebratory and more positive eulogies given at the service? Or was she trying to make the guests at that service feel stupid, to add to their discomfort? What about fairy lights? Light sabers? What was her vision for this day she had clearly imagined in such vivid detail, and where would she leave the instructions so that they would be found?

With so many questions, I wanted to get her on a call as soon as possible, and suggested a few times. Her response came quickly: "I'm so sorry," she said, "I can't speak right now. I'm dealing with a family emergency." Well, of course she was.

At The Oratory Laboratory, the first session we schedule between the speaker and the writer is referred to as the Creative Kickoff, though when you're sitting in the writer's chair, as you are now with me, it precedes the real creative process by quite a distance. In fact, I'd go so far as to say there is nothing creative about it at all. It is in essence a fact-finding, information-gathering mission in which my only concern lies in the external and practical details: who the speaker is, how they arrived at this moment, why they've been singled out to speak, by whom, for whom, where, when, why, and many others, knowing that the answers to my initial questions will define very clearly the ultimate goal of the speech and thus inevitably impact the substance and tone of the draft. I warn clients at the outset that during the meeting they may feel as if they're being interrogated, but in an exciting, revelatory way. Like therapy, though with a gentler resolution—I'm not trying to make anyone cry, yet—and with questions that typically invoke fewer cadavers and less melodrama than Carly's fantasy eulogy. Only once I've identified these details will I ask clients whether they have ideas, half-baked or entirely so, about the subject matter or broad themes of the speech.

When writing your own speech, you might very possibly disregard such simplistic maneuvers and move straight on to tackling the question of what it is you're going to share in your five to fifty minutes of fame. After all, you know perfectly well how you arrived at this moment—who invited you or why you've been obligated to speak. Perhaps the details mentioned above seem too elementary to influence an undertaking of such grand import. Or perhaps the only reason to linger on them at all is to consider how the hell you're going to get out of it—*What a shame, I just signed up for a Tough Mudder the day of, and, you know, it's for charity, so I really can't cancel.* But ignoring the basic facts about the opportunity is another critical error almost as sinful as the YouTube search. Why? Because a great speech is not a personal essay written in tortured seclusion. Nor is it a monologue in a bathroom mirror. It is a well-considered response to a specific set of circumstances, the earliest details of which provide precious clues in defining the central message of your speech, its tone, and its ultimate impact on the audience.

To use a food analogy slightly more profound than a rodent

chef from a Pixar movie: Imagine you're hosting a dinner at home for a bunch of friends. You've got six guests coming on Thursday, and you've seen a recipe you fancy trying out. But then you stop and think about it and you realize that one guest is vegetarian, another is doing the Whole30, and another is your annoying ex who likes to make jokes about how you always keep people waiting. On top of this, your tiny AC unit matches your tiny apartment, it's August, you have a full-time job, and you can only cook one thing at a time in the tiny oven. Oh, and it's Thursday. Now, which sounds better? A whole fish on the bone with herbs and lemon served with four cooked sides complete with sauces and drizzles, or a giant pot of vegetable Thai curry? It's not that one is more delicious in theory, just that one will be a success, the other a shit show. (Personally I'd cancel the dinner—who can be bothered with such fussy eaters?!)

In more prosaic terms, if you're not into cooking or eating (I love the latter and can skip the former), what you end up saying and how you choose to say it is defined to a large extent by the classic questions of *where, why, who*.

> *Where will you be speaking?*
> *Why are you speaking?*
> *Who will be listening?*

Pausing for a moment to reflect on these very pedestrian details and reading into them as you might read tea leaves is always worth the time. (Unlike actually reading tea leaves, which I'm not sure is worth the effort.) The answers will reveal the unchangeable factors that provide both the opportunities and the parameters of a speech. They will tell you how provocative or appeasing you can be with the content and tone, how audacious with your language, and how imaginative with the structure. They tell you to what extent you need to fall in line and respect the precedent of the event or the institution and how far you can push your audience to exceed their expectations. From the sum of their parts a vivid picture will quickly emerge of the kind of speech you're going to be giving. And it is this "creative brief" that will hold you accountable to the needs and desires of all involved throughout the creative process—yours included—no matter how wacky you get with content and tone (and my hope is that you'll get wacky).

In the spirit of the anti-step method, there isn't a correct order in which you should ask these questions (mainly because they all dovetail), only a recommendation from someone who has succeeded for years because I've asked them and contemplated the answers—and failed when I have not. It's a sinking feeling to suddenly realize the day before a speech that you didn't spend long enough considering the *who*. International Women's Day is, after all, not the same as Women's Day.

My process with a client always starts with the *where*, of course, because I typically begin in near total ignorance. At best I have a monosyllabic email stating the exact institution, host, or venue for the speech. At worst I'm sent a vague and rambling explanation of the goal of our engagement, like the email I received the other day asking if I could "rewrite a 4-pager in proper English in the style of TEDx for a kind of SXSW type of event." In proper English I wrote back and asked what the hell that meant.

The *where*, however, pertains less to the physical space

(we'll get to that later) than it does to the forum for the engagement. For example, you might be delivering remarks at your alma mater's annual board meeting, or speaking at a groundbreaking for a new development, or giving a toast at your stepbrother's wedding. The clue often lies in the subject line of the email sent from the host, or the assistant helping you with scheduling, or your agent gently reminding you the book is written but the show is just beginning.

> You're invited to Indira and Peter's wedding!
> Re: Iowa Agricultural Union remarks
> Books of Wonder—book launch/reading

Alone, the forum is not helpful in determining the exact subject of your speech, but it may well reveal plenty about what you're there to do, who's going to be listening, and what they want. A thought leadership summit, for example, immediately signals toward content that educates, enlightens, and inspires an audience of intellectually curious industry insiders. You will want the substance to be well researched, thought-provoking, and sharp. A book launch, on the other hand, will likely require a great deal of personality and anecdote. That said, an industry conference—let's say CES—wants both keynote speakers who have high-level aspirational messaging and speakers who can deliver very targeted, future-focused takeaways. So once you've considered what the forum demands, being very clear on *why* you are speaking is vital. What is the purpose of your particular speech, as you understand it, and what are the expectations for its impact?

While most hosts are delighted just to have locked in another name for the speaker lineup, some can be quite prescriptive about what they want. One of my clients, Sherman, had a very particular job to do. A well-known print artist and collaborator, he invited me to our first meeting at his studio, which housed a collection of just-finished and half-done works by some of the world's most iconic artists. It's one thing to see art hanging in a gallery; it's another to see the paint still drying or the idea in mid-conception. When the widow of an old friend and major philanthropist asked Sherman to give a eulogy for her husband at a major New York institution to be attended by five hundred of the who's who of the modern art scene, she was very sure of why she asked him. "Everyone is going to say how important he was," she had told him. "But you and he had such amazing banter. You were the one he called when he had a joke to tell." Right there, the stakes and the directive were clear: be funny and remind everyone how funny he was. I'm quietly quite proud that one of my collaborations was "exhibited" in a museum of art but I'm more touched by the fact that Sherman called a few weeks later asking for help with another eulogy—this time his mother's. It's a strange thing when someone else's tragedy is a marker for your success, but there it is.

You may, of course, have put yourself up for the job of speaker. In that case you need to be clear why. It can be helpful to think about your objective as a single verb: to educate, to motivate, to celebrate, to incite, to reassure, to enlighten, to introduce, to welcome . . . If you're the maid of honor at your sister's wedding, picking a word may just save you from saying how much you really despise your new brother-in-law. (Celebrate, celebrate, celebrate!) However, the purpose of your speech might require deeper consideration. If you're a politician on the campaign trail, the deliverable might well be to outline your agenda as you move through the country meeting new constituents. But it could be to respond to something that happens while you're crisscrossing the country that requires a very different focus, as was the case for Barack Obama in 2008 when controversial content in sermons given by his pastor, Reverend Jeremiah Wright, surfaced and was circulated by the media. Among other condemnations and grievances, the reverend was quoted as saying "God damn America" and referring to the 9/11 terrorists as "American chickens coming home to roost." In response, Obama needed more than a typical campaign speech. So, while denouncing Wright's comments, he took the opportunity to educate Americans about the very real anger felt by the Black community, and subsequently made one of the most historic speeches on race in America ever. His poll numbers barely flinched.

It may, however, be that a specific purpose has already been defined, not by the host or a sequence of recent events, but by the long-standing traditions and rituals governing the forum or occasion. Commencement speakers are expected to deliver advice or wisdom. The job of the father of the bride is to welcome the guests and talk about his daughter. Weddings happen all over the world all the time. Ergo, a wedding speech has a certain amount of ritual and expectation associated with it.

Now, you can fantasize all you want about the opportunity of speaking at Davos or taking the stage as a dashing best man, but at the end of the day it is the people in the room whose minds and imaginations you hope to enthrall, not your own. In other words, considering the forum and the reason you're there cannot be separated from considering the audience in the room. The *where* and the *why* are inextricably bound to the *who*.

A friend once asked me if I could take a look at a eulogy she'd written for a family member years prior. She'd surfaced it while looking through some old drawers and had been taken aback by how disingenuous she felt it was, given her true feelings about the deceased. She was interested in exploring her relationship to this speech for a master's project and asked for my thoughts. As we jogged together through a sunny New York City park chatting about what her intentions were for such an undertaking, I urged her more than once not to judge herself harshly for what at the time had obviously felt like the right thing to say. Ultimately, I reminded her, a speech isn't necessarily a therapeutic tool. It may be cathartic to put one together, but the product must also respect the needs and desires of its audience.

You might worry that it's inauthentic or manipulative to orchestrate or contrive a message around your audience, but there's another way to think about it. I personally like to believe that public speaking—while it can be exploited by the most egocentric types—is a selfless act of connection. It's how I've learned to be so gentle, patient, and empathetic at home. Seriously. Just ask my family. Throughout this book I will keep returning to the audience as a reminder that the questions you ask yourself along the way must ultimately determine what will electrify the ears, hearts, and minds in the room. The audience not only helps guide the choices you make in regard to tone and language, but also helps you start to identify the kinds of ideas that you might want to share. After all, just as in life, everything you know isn't everything you should say. We are sentient, intelligent beings who constantly modify the parts of ourselves we want to divulge according to the company in which we find ourselves and our surroundings. The same calculations and calibrations should be made for prepared remarks as they are for intimate, spontaneous conversation. You have to consider the audience's interests, their pain points, their awareness, their style, and whether they're aligned in their thinking on your topic or diverse in their opinions. As you navigate through the process, it's a good idea to keep coming back to the audience and asking yourself if the commentary will track with everyone in the room.

When it came to pleasing an audience, the client who perhaps understood this better than anyone was Charlie Angel. Because Charlie was a porn star.

In the early days of The Oratory Laboratory, Nathan and I became acquainted with a veteran TV producer in the dog park of a small Connecticut town. My sister was recovering in the hospital from the birth of her first child, and we had agreed to go up and look after her dogs when she went into labor. There was a Jacuzzi tub in the guest bathroom—could we handle a couple of dogs *and* a new baby? Of course!

One throw of a muddy ball, however, and my niece's arrival was yesterday's news—as the dogs ran and barked at each other we only had ears for our new acquaintance and her talk of TV fame for The Oratory Laboratory. She was convinced a reality series about a husband-and-wife speechwriting team was an easy sell and with connections at all the major networks, she quickly partnered us with a production team in LA to develop a show about what we do. As we thought about how to create a sizzle reel to send to networks, the showrunner mentioned that his college-age niece had recently told him of her plan to invite an adult-film actress to address the small liberal arts college where she was majoring in film studies. They'd been working together on a documentary project for her thesis and, inspired by Charlie's perspective on sex positivity in porn, Edie had won a tough fight with her professors and convinced them to let her bring Charlie in to speak. (They weren't so liberal, it seemed.) Edison's lightbulbs flashed above all of us: we should help the porn star prepare her talk! A collaboration like this couldn't be more sizzling. And so it was that Nathan and I found ourselves on Skype interviewing one of pornography's hottest actresses at the time, Charlie Angel (not her real name nor her real screen name—a pseudo-pseudonym, if you like).

I may regret telling you this, but I really hadn't had all that much involvement with or exposure to porn at that point, which is saying something considering I lived in Spain for two years. My closest brush had been in Vegas during a painstakingly planned West Coast road trip. My best friend and I had spent close to our entire vacation budget renting a ridiculous-looking white convertible that we thought gave us a *Thelma and Louise* edge but in reality probably put us closer to 1980s Fort Lauderdale. Thanks to the rental expense, our lodging along the way had been restricted to scummy hostel room shares with surf bums, religious nomads from Europe, and every other kind of penniless traveler you can imagine with not a topless Brad Pitt in sight. In hindsight, I suppose, arriving in Vegas to find a film crew in the lobby of our hostel shooting a half-naked woman in a stars-and-stripes thong and a man with a large cigar (not a euphemism) and a panama hat was almost so obvious as to have been a cliché. But given the unglamorous location, I was rather surprised to be exchanging my driver's license for a room key with a corny pickup scene playing out in real time behind us. I couldn't help but wonder in which room the denouement would unfold and who might have done what on my bedlinens. We settled into our room—a crusty dormitory with two pairs of bunks, co-inhabited by an eccentric pair of Swedes named Eric and Hans—and by the time we returned to the lobby area to check out the pool, there was nary a butt cheek or nipple in sight.

So, years later, when the Skype video window opened and the call connected, I was surprised by how adorable Charlie was. I don't know what else I was expecting at 5:00 p.m. on a Wednesday, but she looked like anyone at home in the middle of the day might. Curiously, she was clad not in a skimpy stars-and-stripes bikini but a worn-out T-shirt. Neither was she caked in makeup and false lashes. Instead she wore her mousy brown hair in a ponytail, with neat bangs that framed a babyish face devoid of even a trace of mascara. She had a sweet, girl-next-door look—but not in the porno-girl-next-door way. A mountain of laundry in the background added to the innocence and banality of the scene, though I confess I badly wanted to know what was in that laundry hamper. Was that where the patriotic thong was hiding? Or did she prefer 5 for $30 underwear from The Gap? Maybe she wore her boyfriend's tighty-whities. Not wanting to derail the conversation from more pressing items, I jotted down the question for later, below a question about pets.

We knew a little about the context of Charlie's speaking

engagement—that is, we knew where she was speaking, why Edie was bringing her to the school, and what Edie expected of her star guest—but we were curious to hear Charlie speak for herself about what she saw in the opportunity. Why had she agreed to appear and put herself on the line in such an atypical environment for self-expression? What was her motivation, and what was she looking to achieve with her speech? We were also eager to hear her perspective on a controversial topic that had stirred hot debate among feminists since the eighties: the difference between exploitation/oppression and empowerment.

Charlie had a fascinatingly average life story, she told us. Thanks to parents whose only rule when she was a child was not to cross a major road alone, she hadn't experimented all that much with sex or drugs or alcohol while she was growing up. She'd never done anything that landed her in prison, in debt, or in danger (though, unsurprisingly, she did cross that road on her own once). She'd been a nationally ranked college athlete and a scholarship-winning musician with grades good enough to go to medical school had she not prioritized her musical talent. She'd arrived at the idea of porn as a career when a student project led her to examine the relationship between music and sexuality.

She very specifically wanted the students in the room and their teachers to know that she was neither a basket case nor a victim and every bit as smart as any PhD student. She wanted to challenge people's preconceived notions about who she was and what she did and elevate the idea of curiosity. She wanted to take her audience to the crossroads where she'd made a choice: be fearless and follow her curiosity, or allow someone else's outdated moral codes to dictate her life.

In other words, she knew what she wanted her audience to feel, think, know, and to some degree do. A successful speaker controls the narrative while giving the crowd exactly what they want.

But while it quickly became clear that Charlie had a lot to say about her goals for impact, she didn't yet have much of an angle beyond "porn is good." You might say that when the worn-out shirt came off, there wasn't much underneath, both literally and metaphorically. This didn't surprise me much; if she'd had anything more concrete, she wouldn't have needed our help. "Porn is good" was a start, but it wasn't the key takeaway. It would be largely up to us to elaborate on her personal relationship to the issue and help her articulate some of the more nuanced arguments.

Charlie was obviously very good at her job and took a great deal of pleasure in it in every way. Likewise, we were looking forward to applying our skills to the research and composition of her speech—especially Nathan, who had pulled up IMDB before we'd barely even hung up the call. And we had the foundations upon which we knew we would build: the *where*, the *who*, and the *why*.

You might assume that the hallowed halls of an academic institution would be exactly the place for a rigorous debate on pornography, but if Edie hadn't been exaggerating, it sounded as if those in authority had their concerns about the tenor of such a debate when it was originated by someone their bias had led them to pigeonhole. For us, that was an invitation to be as provocative as they were worried Charlie might be. After all, what better place than a liberal arts school to push buttons and open minds? If the professors were nervous about an abrasive delivery or vulgar material, they were in for a treat. Charlie would indeed challenge the audience to question precisely how they viewed the genre and what constituted vulgarity. In our mind, tiptoeing around the practical demands of her job would only prove there was reason to be ashamed or timid. Edie could have chosen anyone in the movie business to come and speak about sex—in my twenties I worked a stint at a very exclusive nightclub in Manhattan and I can think of at least one actress turned activist who enjoyed getting loose in her private booth. Who says a septuagenarian can't wear hot pants? But Edie had recruited Charlie for a reason. Her personal experience in porn was central to the argument.

Before focusing on the audience and how that might further affect the content and tone, we did our due diligence and took a cursory look at the university's roster of speakers from previous years, which indicated no previous record of actors in the pornography genre having given speeches. This gave us carte blanche in terms of the material we could use and how we articulated Charlie's point of view. It's always a smart move to research the venue, institution, or event where you'll be speaking to see what's been done there before and whether it has a reputation or a pattern in terms of the types of ideas and perspectives showcased there. For example, it might once have been very conservative or heavily influenced by an industry and then changed with recent leadership. There may be a certain culture attached to events and rituals, or an inside scoop that helps endear you to the audience and promotes an image of belonging. When it comes to commencements, this is especially true—there is often an unspoken supposition that the speaker will allude to campus buildings, landmarks, and chants. If all these variables seem overwhelming, think of it like this: You receive an invitation to a party in the mail. It's printed in embossed lettering on expensive black card stock, and the envelopes are lined in gold tissue. The details are sparse. Wouldn't you do everything you could to find out who was going, what they'd be wearing, and what you might expect throughout the night? I don't know about you, but I wouldn't want to show up to a cocktail gathering in a penthouse dressed in a Rent-the-Runway Met Gala costume.

Charlie made it clear that the audience's reservations wouldn't hold her back from talking very plainly about the humdrum erotica of her day-to-day life on set. But we knew she had to thread the needle between playing the provocateur and offering an intellectual argument worthy of the scholarly setting. The material would have to meet a certain level of sophistication for a number of reasons, and the forum was just one of them. An additional indicator of how substantive and insightful the speech needed to be was the amount of time for which she'd been given the stage. People often fixate on length, worrying that they don't want to go too long. To this I always ask them about the last time they saw someone timing a speech with a stopwatch. Going on too long only matters if the speech is boring. On the other hand, paying attention to the duration of a speech specified in the invitation is useful in identifying expectations regarding the depth and scope of the themes. Charlie had been given forty minutes followed by a Q&A session, which is a lot of time to fill.

We also wanted to honor Charlie's stated determination to play off the unconscious biases the professors and students alike would inevitably harbor regarding her intelligence, capability, and socioeconomic class. We were willing to guess that the professors would be expecting very little from her, and that motivated us to really blow them away with a lethal combination of tight narrative, powerful data, and well-researched historical context. These elements would be buttressed by conviction and courage, in the form of the intentional use of graphic details, as well as by Charlie's personality: her natural confidence, gentle manner, and eloquence.

When I think about the audience—who is in the room—I'm not just looking at demographics, though of course it's essential to have a grasp of this aspect. I'm thinking about what unites them. Are they all engineers? Are they all mothers? Are they all supremely wealthy? Do they all care about the environment? And what does that say about what they want from the speaker? Charlie would be addressing professors (skeptical and welcoming), but the majority of the audience would be students, many of whom we could assume were decidedly more enthusiastic than the administration was about the prospect of a high-profile porn star visiting their campus. There was a good chance, too, that the hormonal twentysomethings might be "acquainted" with the medium in which Charlie worked, if not familiar with her entire oeuvre in order of release date. But even if their personal experience with Charlie or porn was limited, they would all be eager, no doubt, to see her in the flesh (or clothed, in this case), hear her take on the contrived scenarios often found in porn, and digest some juicy stories about the choices she'd made throughout her career. In the audience there would, no doubt, be people who sat firmly on the other side of the sex-positive feminism debate, so we'd have to work hard to convince them. But either way, the youth demographic gave us permission to lean into the more daring, risqué content to illustrate Charlie's points. The tastes and cultural touchpoints of the younger stakeholders in the room would allow for references and jokes tied to pop culture, college campus life, and other trending topics of the day.

Armed with this detailed information about the context of Charlie's speech, we'd already been able to identify the core messaging, the tone, and the intention. It was going to be a speech about breaking the taboos around sex and pornography. It needed to be both intensely personal and intellectually sophisticated. It would be didactic and passionate. It would include plenty of biographical material baked into a well-researched historical context, touching on key themes such as feminism, prostitution, and morality, to challenge the educators in the room and educate the students. It would require self-awareness and humility in its humor, and bold, direct challenges to the audience. We were ready to get to work on the content, and we knew exactly what kind of material we'd be putting to work.

Had we started without this process, we might not have been so clear on how and where to gather the most interesting material and how to use it. We never would have composed a speech that relayed the details of her double anal scene on the same page as a bit about equal pay. Although I daresay Nathan would still have found time to search Charlie's filmography on IMDB.

2

What's Going On?

The Influence of Physical Environment and Zeitgeist

I've already bought my bathing suit," Sherri told me as we discussed the forum of her speech in greater detail. (You may remember Sherri from the introduction—the astronaut of the GPS theory.) It's not unusual to swap ideas about presentation at the end of a collaboration—I'm all for advising clients on what shoes will keep them from toppling off the stage or which suit will make them feel most powerful. Rarely, however, do we discuss swimwear. But Sherri's speech was to take place in a setting that was light-years away from ordinary.

While analyzing the markers of an event or the host institution can move you further toward the substance and tone of your unwritten remarks, there are still other factors pertaining to the forum to consider. For example, Charlie was to speak at a university, but a more surgical investigation into the setting revealed that she would be addressing a large audience in the main lecture hall. The intentionality behind the content was informed as much by this as it would have been if she'd been giving her talk in, say, the Student Diversity

Committee's office. Our decisions regarding content and tone could have looked very different in a less formal venue.

There is a leap one must take between the abstract requirements of the forum and the purpose and the more tangible, practical characteristics of the moment in question. In other words, when you imagine yourself in the exact physical setting at the exact moment you'll be standing there, what more do you learn? Where exactly are you? What do you see? What just happened in the moments prior? What's happening around you? What's your relationship to the space, if any? These are the finer details on which you need to ruminate—and which you need to consider doubly as hard if you're repurposing a speech you gave six months ago. There are plenty of keynote speakers out there—most often industry pioneers and founders of things—who have been trotting out the same origin-story speech for ten years without enough curiosity to wonder if the tone of the narrative complements the new context in which it's being told.

I myself have fallen victim to such myopia. Way before I'd spent any time thinking about or trying to articulate my creative process, I was invited to speak about public speaking to a gathering of women in technology. It was not a roaring success. I did not do my homework, and having miscalculated the forum and the purpose of my appearance, I rolled in all hot and heavy with a setup joke about high-achieving women and lactation classes. When I learned later that what they had really wanted from me was a workshop on presenting, it dawned on me that neither my breastfeeding joke nor much of the content was appropriate for what turned out to be a seminar for a bunch of twentysomethings in a workplace cafeteria. It probably would have been better to create connection with the seven people who bothered to show up by beginning with a thoughtful question that engaged the group and established trust. I think I established horror.

I first saw this kind of creative dexterity somewhere in my twenties while working for an award-winning Broadway actress and playwright who at the time was an absolute darling of the theater and nonprofit worlds. The cast of characters she'd developed for her hit one-woman show had delighted the likes of Meryl Streep, Melinda Gates, and Michelle Obama. We even went to the White House for a special performance. To lend her talents to more socially conscious causes, she'd also created a separate show in which the same cast of characters performed monologues about disparities in the healthcare system. Between celebrity performances she took this show on the road to organizations such as the Service Employees International Union and hospitals around America, and where she went, I went too.

My job as her assistant was vast in scope. I had to coordinate with the hosts, finalize the contracts, arrange travel, haul her oversized bag of costumes and props around every airport and hotel, and make sure the costumes were pressed and steamed the day of the performance. Having never quite figured out how to iron without burning myself, I wasn't about to experiment with the hotel garment steamers. Hanging the clothes from the shower rod in the bathroom and running the hot water while I watched free cable seemed like a far more sensible way to spend my evening. (It's not as if her show was about the environment.) On top of this, she had very specific needs for travel (holistic nasal sprays, tonics, and lotions) and equally particular instructions when it came to where in the hotel she wanted to sleep and what she did and didn't want to deal with on the day of the show—all of which I facilitated very willingly. After all, she flew me first class everywhere; my air miles account got a real boost. But I also got an education. Cynicism aside, the most precious reward was that in traveling with her and working with her on her scripts, I was exposed for the first time in detail to the frail and inadequate socioeconomic infrastructure on which the country was balancing. Until then, I confess, the very real challenges of so many underserved populations had all but entirely eluded me, and the complexity of the solutions was not something I understood. As she described the real health consequences of institutional racism—overpolicing, a barely livable wage—and the effects of daily cortisol-releasing stress, the value of a barbershop and its impact on health in the community, I learned to appreciate how important it was for her to speak to each individual audience—whether in Genesee County or Louisville—as personally and empathetically as possible.

Before every show she insisted I research the audience and the host organization, any historical points of interest related to the setting, and any recent newsworthy stories in the community. For every show, she would tweak each character's monologue to make sure she was speaking directly to the people in the room and within the cultural moment we found ourselves in. The first character to "show up" would always make a humble introduction to the "friends" she had brought with her to speak. In this opening gambit she'd make sure to give a nod to her environment, referencing a contemporary local issue, a familiar place, and a common complaint—all in character. When we were in Hawaii, for example, her Jewish bubbe was

shvitzing under the palm trees. She never assumed that just because her show was a hit she didn't need to respect every event
as unique and every audience as one to win over.

Years later—and with my failed women-in-tech seminar an
unfortunate blip in the rearview mirror—by the time Sherri
and I got around to discussing two-pieces versus one-pieces,
we had worked together many times with the same painstak-
ing focus on every aspect of the forum, the audience, and
the physical setting. Our very first collaboration had been
a keynote in honor of Sherri's receipt of a highly prestigious
women-in-science award. Before embarking on the speech I'd
done the obligatory creepy sweep of the internet to find out
who this space cadet was and discovered to my amazement
that, just as Charlie had challenged my expectations of a porn
star, Sherri, with her cascading blond hair and California tan,
was far more glamorous and zhuzhed than I would have expected of an aeronautical engineer. This lingering stereotype
of bespectacled, unfeminine science nerds is what comes of
not seeing enough women in STEM when I was growing up,
I suppose.

Sherri's speech was to be delivered at a famous planetarium, the same one to which, as a high school space geek,
she'd driven her parents' beat-up Oldsmobile in order to attend lectures. She could immediately draw a line from that
wishful teenager to the humble award recipient standing at
the podium on the night of the gala. From there we addressed a European audience at a festival for tech innovators.
After that she spoke to the media and local officials about
her first trip to space in a civilian rocket ship she'd helped
design—and the speech took place on the tarmac outside the
spacecraft's hangar. There was always a new audience, a new

forum, and a different setting. And so there was always a new look at what we thought she should say and how.

For our fifth collaboration, Sherri had been asked to share her story about her mission at a gathering of nongovernmental organizations and nonprofits hosted every year by a famous philanthropist. That might sound stuffy; however, the setting was anything but. Sherri would deliver the remarks, she told me, during one of several evenings spent at a private beach residence. After we'd giggled like teenagers about how fun that would be, we discussed the implications of such a mise-en-scène. At this stage in the itinerary the guests would have already spent a couple of days getting to know each other through water sports, guided adventures, cocktails, and facilitated conversation. Sherri would be speaking in an open-air gazebo with a gentle sea breeze blowing around a slightly tipsy group of linen-clad nonprofiteers—people with whom she would have recently forged new friendships while riding the waves on a jet ski and sipping mango daiquiris poolside.

When we looked at the audience and the forum in a vacuum, we could make certain assumptions about the type of narrative that would draw them in. They weren't in it for a sound bite. This was a 501(c)(3) crowd. UN ambassador types. Nonprofit warriors. Sherri's fellow speakers were covering topics that ranged from the refugee crisis to the future of wind energy, so we quickly decided the right thing to do was to focus on the impact of civilian space travel on global relationships, environmental issues, and humanity. And given the setting, however we stitched that story together, it would need to come off the page with a heightened sense of intimacy and informality. She couldn't prowl the stage prompting the people in the room to "imagine a feeling you've never felt before," as a TED speaker might command their audience. I pictured her standing or even sitting on a high stool with a handheld microphone. Any big ideas and thesis statements would need to be packaged as humble hunches rather than as bold declarations. The tone had to be more confessional than didactic. She could use notes, yes, but the material had to feel natural enough that she could rely less on her script than she would typically have done up on a podium. You'll hear plenty later on how I feel about using scripts. Ple-e-e-e-nty. But for now, my point is only that taking into account the exact environment was a crucial step in thinking about what material to use and how to use it.

Analyzing your physical setting might feel like a more precise and specific answer to the question of where you will be speaking, but you should also be aware that setting, as defined by traditional storytelling, incorporates the cultural and historical moment too. Imagine a title card at the start of a movie: *Cairo, 1947* or *London, yesterday*. Capturing the zeitgeist is a way to anchor the speech in its cultural moment and imbue it with the power of relevance. Describing the news as "fake" now, for example, has an implication it might not have had prior to the 2016 US presidential election.

There's a brilliant example of how Martin Luther King Jr. and his speechwriting partner Clarence B. Jones reconstituted a famous passage from his 1963 "I Have a Dream" speech four years later in an entirely different context and with a wholly distinct message. In 1963 Dr. King stood before the Lincoln Memorial and declared: "With this faith we will be able to transform the jangling discords of our nation into a beautiful symphony of brotherhood." Beyond the poetry of the discords and the symphony, his words resonated with optimism and promise. The future tense in "we will" signaled a certainty beyond possibility. King, however, had always been an impassioned advocate for social justice and economic fairness and had very specific views on African American participation in and exploitation by society. Four years after his "I Have a Dream" speech, he delivered a stinging rebuke of the Vietnam War in a far bigger and more wide-ranging speech. Jones pulled the "discord" line and altered it ever so slightly for this new moment. His friend the preacher would now say: "If we will make the right choice, we will be able to transform the jangling discords of our world into a beautiful symphony of brotherhood." The line now rested on a condition about a "right choice," and as he aimed his message squarely at the US government, the discords for which they were now responsible had expanded to encompass the whole world. Those same words that had inspired so many millions would now piss off a lot of the same people. It makes me wonder if he and Jones intentionally used the same verbiage to test the audience and hold them accountable, almost as if saying, *You liked those words when it suited you, didn't you?* Either way, it shows you how thoughtful repurposing can revitalize previously used material with new power in a different moment and for a different crowd.

Not to equate Dr. King with Tinder, but as a segue on the significance of the cultural moment: When I started writing speeches for other people's weddings, dating apps hadn't been invented yet, and if the couple had met on OkCupid, it was categorically out of bounds for the speech. Nowadays, someone's Tinder profile provides a well of potential joke material, so much so that I try not to rely on it for fear it's become too much of a trope. I hope I never have to write a speech about star-crossed lovers who spotted each other for the first time on Zoom's Gallery View during a company-wide meeting. That would be truly depressing. But I would hope that if I closed my eyes and pointed to a speech selected at random out of the hundreds I've written, even an amateur detective would be able to skim the document and then place it in time on account of its references.

I remember a few years ago I worked with a high-powered entertainment executive on a commencement speech she would be delivering at an HBCU (a historically Black college or university). We'd worked together years prior on a birthday speech and it had gone well, but she was nervous about this invitation. First, she was billed to speak on the same day as a major celebrity; that didn't intimidate her, but as she saw it, it relegated her to "supporting act." On top of this, she'd chosen a non-HBCU herself for college but was very close socially with several alumni of this particular school, so she felt added pressure to show reverence for the graduates. And third, like most people, she didn't fancy the idea of being live-streamed on the internet while speaking to thousands of people on the most important day of their lives so far.

Making a speech should take you on a journey of personal growth, so it will not come as a shock that every speech I write takes me on a journey of learning too. This commencement was no exception. Having been educated in London and Bristol, I'm only now becoming familiar with the American education system as I wrestle the New York City Department of Education on my children's behalf. I still don't know how old an eighth grader is or what's considered a decent grade point average. More importantly, I'm white, so my inherent frame of reference was automatically off kilter with my client's. Not only did I have to learn about the college at which she was speaking, its different programs, and the schools whose students would graduate that particular day, but I needed to immerse myself very quickly and thoughtfully in the history and traditions associated with both this school and HBCUs in general. Needless to say, I felt pressure to support her to the best of my ability, knowing ability alone might not be enough. I leaned heavily on my client for her perspective and insight; I also talked to other friends and professionals who had attended HBCUs, I watched a lot of footage of the school's acclaimed marching band, and then I decided that watching Beyoncé's documentary *Homecoming* in the middle of the day (for the third time) could absolutely be justified as research.

In the end we decided that the peaks and troughs of Maya's own story provided proof of a central point: that it's in the very places you don't belong where you find the power to create the greatest change. We grounded the larger takeaways in her own experience as an executive in the entertainment industry, anticipating that the students would enjoy hearing about a powerhouse company responsible for churning out hits they knew and loved. The graduates would enjoy hearing about how, with the cards stacked against her, she'd risen to the highest echelons. And enjoy it they did, she told me afterward, relieved to have received such positive feedback from the dean and other attendees.

But I thought about the speech again some time later as I watched a Howard University commencement speech for research in the summer of 2020, and I reflected on what Maya's speech would have been had she asked me to help her months into a global pandemic and weeks after the video of George Floyd's murder sparked a global movement of protest against systemic racism. Would we have written the same speech? I highly doubt it.

I can get a sense of when that speech was penned simply from the callouts to specific contemporary trending artists. But in 2020, with Black Lives Matter protesters and their allies marching on the streets of every American city, a rallying cry to keep showing up in the places you don't belong would have taken center stage with even more force and significance in the narrative. Given the moment, Maya's own stories would have set the stage for the theme, but they'd have then cleared the way for contemporary examples of activism and protest, the broader underpinning of the cultural, political, and social climate, and an exploration of the way students right there in that moment were seeking out those spaces of discomfort.

It also occurred to me that had Maya been speaking in 2020, she'd have had to compete with Beyoncé herself, who, along with Barack Obama, addressed the entire graduating class of 2020 in streamed video speeches. When the whole world moved inside and video speeches became the only way to deliver public remarks, it opened a Pandora's box of previously unknown challenges: How many camera angles works best? What's the background? Where is the speaker in the frame? Cult filmmaker John Waters delivered a hilarious commencement address early on in the pandemic to the students of the School of Visual Arts New York City. He stepped up to a podium with his notes, in front of a velvet curtain projected on a green-screen background, and had it filmed just as if he were facing a live crowd. Queen Bey, however, and President Obama spoke to the camera, a hidden tele-prompter nearby giving them a clean eyeline straight to the viewer. Video speeches nowadays are so much more than just a recording of a speaker on a TED stage posted online. When you're addressing a camera rather than a live crowd, the possibilities are endless.

Video has been around forever, but I believe its potential as a way to address audiences, large and small, has yet to be truly explored and exploited. I was impressed when the queen (of England's) annual Christmas address to the nation—highly anticipated by the octogenarian-plus population—got a makeover a few years ago. During the updated televised version the picture cut away from the queen at her desk to footage of all the royal weddings and births and happenings of the past year. It played like a short film. Cory Booker gave Americans something similar when he announced in 2019 that he was throwing his hat into the ring as a presidential candidate. Rather than make a speech at a podium and invite the press, he ran what felt more like a digital ad. Off cam-era, Booker's energetic vocals provided the narrative, while the audience watched montages of stills and footage from his childhood, his community, and his political experience. More recently I had a lot of time for rapper Megan Thee Stallion's *New York Times* opinion piece—a striking video whose mes-sage, narrated by its author and artfully illustrated on film, dealt with the reality of being a woman of color in America.

Canadian communication theorist Marshall McLuhan famously coined the phrase "The medium is the message." In doing so, he implied that every medium creates different opportunities for storytelling. For example, adapting a book to film would inevitably require a rewriting of the story in the book. Likewise, a radio adaptation is written differently than a theater piece and yes, a speech is written and delivered to an audience in a different way than a feature-length essay on the same topic would be. In this way, the medium of video creates an entirely different setting for a speech than a stage or a microphone would, and therefore cannot be overlooked during the early stages of this process.

Despite your distance from the audience, you're potentially beaming into a more private space, and in that sense you are far more intimate with the audience than you've ever been. How does that affect the way you communicate your message? Are you more casual and conversational? Or are you more direct and economical with your words knowing that it may be harder to get them to focus? What about length? Are you tempted to shorten your address knowing that their attention spans in this more personal setting may be compromised, and if not, how do you keep the viewers engaged throughout? What are people used to seeing on video as a medium? Graphics? Music? Is sitting in front of a screen talking enough to keep viewers from their phones or iPhoto?

A friend in advertising recently observed that since his whole company had transitioned to Zoom for meetings and client presentations, a number of young dynamic presenters who had once been very quick on their feet and nimble when it came to reading the room in person were lifeless on video. He complained that now they were at home "hiding" behind a screen, it appeared they'd started scripting their presentations, and in doing so had lost spontaneity and connection. Disappointed by this professional neglect and lack of imagination, he asked if I had any advice that he could pass on to improve their technique. The way I see it, the problem wasn't that they were scripting their remarks. The issue was laziness. They weren't working hard enough to take advantage of the new medium in creating connection with the people on the other side of the screen. On video, just as in person, but especially when your head has been severed from your body, energy and connection with the audience are everything and you must use all the technology at your disposal to deliver that to the audience. It doesn't matter if you scripted your remarks if your microphone and camera technique are terrible. It could be the best presentation in the world and it still wouldn't matter.

The most common misconception is thinking that on Zoom you should be more subdued or less active than you might aim to be in a physical environment. If you are someone who becomes physically energized when you present, don't go changing! But maybe you want to set yourself back from the screen with a good HD camera and a good microphone. This way you'll avoid distorting the audio for everyone with your enthusiastic manifesto about "what Gen Zers really care about" over crappy laptop speakers. You might also want to create a bit of an environment, with a well-designed background that tells a story about who you are and what kind of atmosphere you're trying to create.

Most importantly, though, if you're flying solo at home without a sophisticated tech team from an online event crew to provide a prompter, you will want to think about where to put your notes. This detail is key because whether you're delivering a live presentation or a set of pre-taped, prepared remarks, connecting with the audience on the other side of the camera relies almost entirely upon how you make eye contact and the direction of your gaze. On camera, when you're sitting so close to a screen, the slightest shift of your gaze is traceable, unless you turn up wearing shades, which . . . is a choice, I suppose, if you're pitching the Miami tourism board. With such close proximity to your audience, reading from speaker notes beneath your deck of slides or note cards placed on your desk, for example, will look awkward and feel evasive—like a guilty child lying about who yanked the cat's tail. So what's the solution? I highly recommend multiple monitors so that when you are using a script or typed notes, or even if you're leading clients through a screen share of a Prezi, the monitor with the text you're reading can be placed closest to your camera, ensuring your eye line meets that of your audience, even if you're not looking directly at their faces. You can then position a separate screen where your audience is just to the side or behind—anywhere you can get a sense of their reaction. It's all about creating an in-home studio setup that works for you so that you're as comfortable in the setting as you would be if you'd checked the height of the podium, the microphone, and the AV specs before taking the stage to address a crowd of hundreds at a conference.

It can take a lot of experimentation to get it right, but as you examine the medium of video for a speech and its impact on your choices, just don't forget that while you may be sitting in a remote and isolated room, thinking you're off the hook and you don't have to try as hard, you're far from alone and your audience wants you to be just as fabulous as they'd expect from the IRL you. (I had to use the lingo and show off my tech bona fides somewhere.)

Despite the discomfort many people feel with the medium, I don't believe that speaking on video limits us; rather, it offers a new frontier of innovation in public address. Organizers of online events should take this into consideration. I've worked on enough digital galas and conferences to know that decisions concerning what the audience sees and hears during talks and in between can dramatically heighten the overall experience. In fact, one of these events was due to take place on the very same island as Sherri's speech until it was canceled because of the Covid-19 pandemic. The organizers scrambled to try to re-create the summit online until I, and the design team with whom I was working, pointed out that you can't simply re-create a barstool in a Caribbean gazebo on a computer. As a speaker confronting the challenge of making public remarks on camera, the attention to detail should be no different. The bathing suit can wait till next time.

3

I Think Therefore
I Am (in the Speech)

Identifying a Main Character in
Your Narrative

I don't want to talk about my breakdown," Maggie told me very pointedly. She was due to speak at a big gala hosted by one of New York City's most prestigious cultural institutions—a museum she had helped establish—and I'd asked conversationally as an icebreaker what she'd been up to in the last three years. She'd exiled herself in Europe, she told me, to recover from a bout of exhaustion and depression brought on by years of tireless devotion to the charitable causes related to the museum.

We agreed her nervous breakdown wasn't essential for the speech. Not great messaging for the donors in the room. But Maggie's reticence extended beyond a desire for privacy. She was the unwilling hero in her own tale, determined to deflect any attention at all away from her personal life.

In traditional storytelling you can tie yourself in knots trying to pull apart and distinguish the concepts of protagonist, main character, and hero from each other. Master classes abound relating to the definitions of these and the importance

of one versus the others. Reduced to their most basic transla-
tions: the protagonist is the character whose decisions drive
the story forward; the main character (who might also be the
protagonist) is the character whom these choices impact and
from whose point of view we often experience the story;
and the hero (who could also be the protagonist and the
main character) is a character who undergoes a major transformation during a journey. If even this explanation leaves
you scratching your head in confusion, don't worry too
much. The reason I bring it up at all is that at a certain point,
the question of why you are speaking becomes a question of
why *you* are speaking, and the role you play in the narrative
you're about to construct suddenly becomes a crucial point
to get right.

A speech isn't a story. It's a narrative framework inside of
which lots of small stories and thoughts and fragments combine to form something much bigger. (Stop scratching; I'll
unpack this idea more later.) And as a speaker, you are also
the author. If you were the pedantic type, you might assert
that this automatically positions you as the main character,
if not the protagonist too. But sharing a perspective or an idea
doesn't necessarily mean that your feelings, stories, and experiences are central to the narrative. So as you build this
framework you need to get straight at the outset how "main"
your character really is, to know what sources to use for the
content. You might well not feature in the action as much as
you think—a concept that has come as a welcome relief to
many of my clients, and a nasty shock to others. Once, a long
time ago, I wrote an email to a mother of the groom whose
insistence on lingering on her own nuptial melodramas as

we crafted the speech was exasperating. I thought that I had done a commendable job of explaining very gently that the speech wasn't about her and she needn't focus so much on apologies and excuses for what she deemed as her failures. Up until then we'd been getting on very well and she'd been very happy with our work. At that point, however, she called me rude and asked for her money back.

At The Oratory Laboratory when I'm training new writers, I make an early distinction between speeches about people and speeches about things or ideas. In one, the subject of the speech is clearly defined at the outset as someone else. There's no better indicator of your role than that. It's about someone else! Whether it's the bride, the deceased, or the bravely married forty years later, your objective is to celebrate them. You're the one with the job not because of anything you've done other than knowing them better than most other people in the audience or knowing them in a different context than the person who'll be speaking before you. As best man, you may well feature in many of the juicy anecdotes, and posit your own theories about the groom's redeeming qualities and not-so-charming habits, but the point of those anecdotes is to highlight his characteristics and idiosyncrasies. No one cares about how long you've known him or what your very special relationship is like; they're interested in what you know about him as a result. They don't care that you used to play soccer on weekends together; they want to know about the signed Ronaldo shirt he wore every time but never washed. *A speech about someone else simply cannot be a speech about you.*

Where this point gets a little murkier is when a speaker wants to express the impact someone has had upon them as proof of their extraordinary value—a husband to his wife of twenty-five years, for example, or a mourner touching on the enduring legacy of a friend. Of course there is space in a speech about someone else to illustrate the impression of their love on your life, but it is always better when the impact reflects the character of that person rather than elaborates on a story of personal transformation for you. Couples looking to compose their own vows illustrate this balancing act beautifully, regardless of what shape these intimate remarks take.

There are several ways in which I'm able to collaborate with almost-weds in helping them express their commitment in their own way. One approach is what I loosely refer to as the "individual" version, where I work with one or both parties and we craft something unique and unassociated with the other's piece in its content and structure. In this execution, the content is very much geared toward the qualities of the other person, but it also includes reflection on the ways the betrothed has changed the speaker's life in some wonderful manner and a statement of their intent as a response. Which isn't as contractual and litigious as it sounds. What I mean is that, like conventional vows, they articulate in some way a promise or a set of promises. In this way, when compared to the bride or groom's speech at dinner later, the speaker would indeed be speaking about themselves far more. Which, when you think about it, makes perfect sense, since after all the vows are just for one person. The guests are witnesses, onlookers in an intimate dialogue in which they do not feature. This is the key distinction that allows the speaker to be very open and forthcoming about their feelings. Though a marriage is a public act, the vows are not crafted with an audience in mind. They're singular in this way, though I do still like to include humor, since if a bunch of people have to listen, why not make it fun for them too?

The alternative to the "individual" option is to craft a structure for both sets of vows and customize them within the same framework, as I did with Andrea and Suki. Andrea was a hot dance teacher and free spirit. Her fiancée, Suki, was far straighter than she was—an earthy, more stable type with an office job. Their compatibility was built on their differences as much as their shared values, something we made sure to capture throughout the ceremony. In working with their friend on the officiant's address as well—church leaders are so last century—we played on the couple's dueling qualities:

> *If you ask Andrea what dancing with Suki is like, she will tell you that Suki likes to lead because it comes naturally to her. She'll also tell you that that's okay because she always knows just how to hold her and that somehow she makes every single dance as romantic as the first they shared.*
>
> *If you ask Suki what dancing with Andrea is like, she'll tell you stuff that I probably shouldn't repeat at a wedding ceremony.*

When it came to the vows, Andrea loved the idea of having me write both hers and Suki's, and we agreed it would be best to keep them secret from each other so that they would create maximum impact on the day. So I spoke to both of them separately and sent them their own questionnaires, and with the answers I crafted a skeleton that I fleshed out with the details they shared with me about each other. Such a structure meant they could speak about the other's qualities very specifically and then make the first-person vow to echo these qualities. For example:

> *Andrea, over the past 1,364 days, you've made me feel like the most important person in your world. When I say I like a certain type of cuisine, you've booked a restaurant. If I mention a show, you've bought the tickets. If I look in a store, you've ordered my size. I do try not to do that too often.*
>
> *I promise you that I will always listen to you the way that you listen to me and to pay attention to your needs and desires.*

Of course, wedding speeches are not all quite so humble. I've also worked with people whose idea of expressing gratitude to their bride or groom is to talk about themselves for ten minutes first. If I had to call out the culprit most guilty of self-centered storytelling, it would be, without question, the father of the bride. Especially if he happens to be wealthy and successful. Time and time again I've observed men of distinction completely unable to disentangle their successes from the accomplishments and agency of their children.

My favorite chauvinist, Paul, had a story better suited for the locker room of an all-men's country club than for his daughter's wedding. Nathan and I met Paul in his office, wood-paneled and adorned with pictures of the family on yacht vacations as well as trophies for his sporting triumphs. Within minutes of ushering us, his captive audience, to our seats, he regaled us with a story about his daughter's birth.

He'd been at a Mets game when he got a call from his wife to say she was going into labor and heading to the hospital. Damn, he'd thought, this game was just getting good. So he waited until the bottom of the second inning hoping that things might move along quickly in the labor room and he'd get a call when it was "go time." Eventually, when his wife's contractions were no longer manageable and through gritted teeth, cursing his name, she made the doctors call him, he jumped in a car to the hospital. (I actually have no idea how her labor went; maybe she was drugged up and oblivious, but as a mother of two with a good memory of the excruciating pain of childbirth and only a little resentment of the injustice of the biological burden, I'm taking artistic and maternal liberty for effect.) And yet, as she screamed her way to delivery, Paul was not bedside but glued to the game on TV in the waiting room. When the baby arrived he had just enough time to give a hug to mother and child, admire how "gorgeous" the baby was—it was his after all—and make it back to Queens for the top of the ninth. His team won! I listened with incredulity to this account, and then when I was able to gather myself I asked: "Are you and your daughter's mother still married?" The answer, of course, was no.

Though the story itself was, technically speaking, very strong, in that it had a great beginning, middle, and end, the stakes were high, and the characters were forever altered by the end (the mother especially, oy!), I could not recommend that Paul go in this direction. It made him sound as if he thought he was a hero—the perfect incarnation of the alpha male—when actually it just made him sound like a self-absorbed asshole. He insisted on using it, however, embellishing it further with every draft. Eventually, after the second draft, we parted ways, unable to get on the same page about that and the rest of his material, which included a story about how their infant daughter was a total buzzkill on their date nights because she'd cry during dinner at the fancy restaurant they'd take her to and then apparently didn't stop crying until she was seven. I wasn't surprised, really. Paul made me want to cry.

The fatal mistake Paul made was that his story did not serve his subject; it only served to massage his own ego. But it didn't have to be this way. He could have told it with a different goal. There is a way to write even a first-person story and still make the subject of it the main character. When my grandmother turned ninety I kicked off my speech at her birthday dinner with a personal story very much composed in the first person and yet entirely generous in function. The opening went like this:

> When I was a young girl at Ken High there were a few things I liked to boast about to my friends. Being the only child in the school with an orthodontic plate rated very highly on my list of achievements. Having a birthday on a leap year was buzzworthy for sure. But most of all I liked to tell people how old my grandmother was. "She's sixty-four," I would tell people, even when they didn't ask. "But that's not all," I would add. "She has the energy of a twenty-one-year-old." I didn't necessarily know any twenty-one-year-olds or how much energy they had, but I heard Mum say it and decided it sounded right. My friends' grannies were all ailing old biddies by comparison. Mine was a firecracker. A Scottish one at that. She walked for miles every day, she operated a pedalo like it was an Olympic sport, and she ran back and forth be-

tween the kitchen and the dining room table more times in one day than Caroline goes to Whole Foods, and that's saying something.

For years Grandma just hovered at sixty-four, never even vaguely approaching the Beatles' idea of what that might look like. Because she never aged in body or mind, I don't think I paid much attention to whether she was aging on paper. And I think a good twenty years passed before I asked Mum, "How old IS Grandma?"

The story was a recollection of mine and I drove the narrative, but the takeaway was undeniably about my grandmother's longevity. She's ninety-three as I write this. Or is she ninety-four? . . . There is so much to love about my grandmother, and I think I can safely say that in this speech I made it abundantly clear how important she was to me and to her family at large. But that said, there is only so much sentimental gushing I would do in a speech even about my granny at an intimate family dinner. When I convey feelings about someone in a speech, it's always because I've worked bloody hard to outline all the reasons why they are so special first. You can call me unemotional and British if you want. I can take it. I know a good musical makes me cry. But I do believe that any misty-eyed declaration of love or admiration that isn't attached to a noble trait or feature about a person can be saved for a bathroom confessional over a shared box of tissues later in the evening (if that's your thing).

It comes back to this plain truth: the speech is for the audience, not just for the friend you're speaking about, and it's not meant to prove that you love them the most. The worst offenders pile onto this self-satisfying behavior by using corny lines such as "She's like a sister to me" that put the bride in the speaker's orbit rather than vice versa. I understand the desire to express that kind of closeness, but I know it's my job to make the speaker feel as if she's conveying her love without having to verbally abuse the audience with such clichés. I always tell my children, "Actions speak louder than words." Yes, revolutionary parenting. But in speechwriting, the same applies. If you have taken the time to craft an extraordinary speech about how wonderful your brother or sister or your best friend is, that is one of the purest expressions of love and gratitude. Don't cheapen it with self-serving, emotionally saturated drivel.

I talked earlier of the two types of speeches. When it comes to speeches about things—be they cocktails, incarceration, betrayal, remote learning, or the future of air travel—it can be tricky to decipher how personal the material has to be in order to achieve likability and loyalty from the audience. Unlike wedding vows, a speech is not a soliloquy but something akin to the moment in a conversation in which one person is doing most of the talking. Where my British reluctance to over-emote serves me well in speeches about people, there are plenty of occasions where withholding your own personal experiences can be detrimental to the relationship you build with the audience. Self-deprecation—another culturally inherited trait—can be charming, but not if it stands in the way of your ability to emotionally connect.

In order to understand how me, me, me a speech might be, be, be, I revisit everything I've learned so far about the event, the expectations, and the purpose. The expectations as implied by the invitation or the obligation speak volumes about the role of the speaker in the narrative. A creative director asked to present on the rise of e-commerce, for example, should not anticipate making themselves the central character. Oprah, on the other hand, might well be expected to tie her own personal experiences into a speech celebrating minority business leadership. And yet if she were to take the stage to accept a lifetime achievement award, her remarks would almost certainly be more deferential to others in her story or those who would be touched by the category of her award. The "I" would be restricted to notes of gratitude.

The purpose of the speech is a vital clue to how much of your own story can overshadow a larger theme or point, but—frustratingly—the nuances are still more abundant. So beyond the event parameters, I look at the relationship and dynamic of the speaker to the audience in the moment. A speaker might have conceived of a topic or theme they think is a stunning and powerful idea for their speech, but I always ask whether it's going to satisfy the people listening in that unique venue and moment. The formidable TV producer Shonda Rhimes delivered one of my all-time favorite speeches about women's achievement at the Sherry Lansing Leadership Awards ceremony in 2014. But her 2016 turn on the TED stage was hugely disappointing. I think she intended for the piece to reveal her flaws as a parent and invite connection with the audience, but she never really exposed any pain or conflict. Instead, an unoriginal idea—"My Year of Saying Yes"—was couched in an uncomfortably self-satisfied narrative about her big-shot Hollywood life. And this from a huge admirer who would love to write speeches for her and likely now never will. Sorry, Shonda. Call me?

Personal stories for inspiration and relatability can bring an industry leader's idea or theory to life. And sure, if the speaker is famous, they can of course satiate an audience hungry for the inside scoop or a look inside the mind and life of someone they admire. But as I'm gathering material and putting together a first draft, I try to put myself in the seated audience while wearing the speaker's shoes by asking, *Is this what I hoped to hear from this particular individual, today and in this setting?* An intellectually thirsty TED audience is not equivalent to an audience at, say, a motivational retreat, where Rhimes's very personal speech may have been more appropriate. At another type of event the speaker may be representative of something bigger—a movement, a cause, or a larger body of people. If so, the "I" may manifest more often as "we." The personal becomes the collective. Or maybe the audience doesn't care as much about who the speaker is as they do about what they've learned and what they know.

Let's take two reality TV stars, for example. And in the spirit of "Rhimes," let's call them Ben and Ken. Ben and Ken are both influencers in the lifestyle space and they have each been invited to deliver the keynote at separate events. Ben is asked to speak at an annual gathering hosted by a large corporate entity unrelated to his area of expertise. The host has indicated that Ben can talk about whatever he wants, but that the intended outcome is aspirational—his audience are trying to climb the corporate ladder as he once was. So we decide that his speech can be underpinned almost entirely by the chronological retelling of his own personal journey to success. It happens to be a magnificent story full of hair-raising plot twists and absurd characters that would be better suited to a Guy Ritchie flick, so we decide not much more is needed besides a high-level setup and a moral at the end of the tale about faking it till you make it.

I Think Therefore I Am (in the Speech)

At the time of our collaboration, Ken is a well-known name in his field too, but not yet the screen star he is today as a cast member in one of TV's most popular reality shows. He's been asked to speak at an industry-specific event to be attended by his peers in the field. His relative fame within his trade is clearly less important than what he knows about it. So we set up Ken's theme with an equally fascinating personal account and then devote the remaining 70 percent of the speech to the truths, data, and opinions that his story underscores. Two guys doing the same thing, but at different positions on the hero spectrum. I'd love to work with Ken again now and flesh out his tell-all celebrity story as I did with Ben. There are plenty of great moments of ingenuity and professional recklessness that would contribute well to an engrossing "I made it and here's how" speech for the appropriate audience. And I'm dying to ask what he thinks of Ben—are they friends or archrivals vying for the limelight on the People Magazine Awards red carpet?

Commencement speeches, while uniform in what they expect from the speaker, offer an even clearer picture of how difficult the decision can be about how far to weave your experiences into the advice. And they perfectly illustrate why I will go to my grave saying there is no right way to do this job of speechwriting. To me, commencement addresses are the hardest speeches to write because they assume that in somewhere between ten and forty minutes the speaker will deliver something thoughtful, inspiring, and really smart (because, you know, the audience has just graduated), as well as funny (because the audience is in celebration mode). It's such a high bar. When I'm writing a commencement speech I have to keep reminding myself of something J. K. Rowling said in her graduation speech at Harvard. (This was back in 2011 when people still liked her and Harry Potter and the LGBTQ community had only wizards and cosplay in common.) Rowling said: "Delivering a commencement address is a great responsibility. Or so I thought. Until I cast my mind back to my own graduation. The commencement speaker that day was the distinguished British philosopher Baroness Mary Warnock. Reflecting on her speech has helped me enormously when writing this one, because it turns out I can't remember a single word she said."

One of my favorite speeches in the commencement category was delivered by US women's soccer champion Abby Wambach at Barnard College. I watched it and wished I'd written it because I felt so in tune with the way it was pieced together structurally, like one of those crazy origami mobiles that, when you pull it out of the box, unfolds into a perfect sculpture—one shape interlocked with the next, various elements sticking out but held tightly together by the thread in the middle. Wambach moved smoothly between personal anecdotes, fairy-tale metaphors, and scientific discoveries, from statements to hard data, from upbeat slogans to call-and-response challenges. There was so much of Abby's own story in there, and each recollection or anecdote brought with it a teachable moment to share with the graduates. In her speech, "I" became "you" and often turned into "we." It was inclusive and delivered on the promise of advice and personal revelation that all audiences want from their heroes and icons. And Wambach was right in the middle, a first-person narrator with a meaty message of female strength and comradeship hung on the bones of her own experiences.

But then you have a commencement speaker like Princeton University professor Keeanga-Yamahtta Taylor, who used her platform at Hampshire College to call the graduates to activism, painting a stirring and provocative picture of the state of the world and outlining where their generation might find the inspiration, hope, and desire to create change. Taylor opened the speech with a witty confession that she'd applied as a high school senior to Hampshire and didn't get in. "It's good to finally be here," she said to laughter. But very quickly her speech turned serious as she lambasted then president Donald Trump and the dangerous path she believed the country was on. Taylor wasn't a mere talking head; the ideas and opinions expressed within the speech were hers, but she presented them as fact and talked to the audience as "you." In fact, she laid out her plan at the top: "I'm not here to tell you what to do with your lives, but I will tell you what I think is necessary to be in this world that we live in right now." She then went on to describe that world before offering the students some ideas of what to do in it. As an organizer, Taylor spoke more broadly on behalf of communities across America who felt the same way. She was there not as a celebrity to impart secrets she'd learned but as a concerned citizen worried about what might lie ahead. Though her tone and her delivery were imbued with the kind of passion that clearly exposed the personal sacrifices she'd made to a greater cause, the narrative was not in any way shaped around stories in which she was the central character.

If we were to use a soccer analogy to describe the way each of the previous two speakers takes center stage in the narrative, Wambach would be the midfielder who wows the crowd with a few brilliant pieces of footwork and then passes the ball forward to her teammate to take a shot at goal, whereas

Taylor would be the epitome of the workhorse defender, ensuring victory by keeping the ball away from the opponent's possession near her team's goal and surrendering any personal glory in the effort. They both bring equal value to the game; one is not better than the other. Then there's the hotshot striker who hangs on to the ball for too long, thinking they can take a shot at goal too, only to realize at the last minute they can't and it's too late to make a successful pass.

Unfortunately in the case of her commencement speech in New Hampshire, this describes Disney's chief creative officer and writer of the *Frozen* franchise, Jennifer Lee, with whom I became briefly obsessed after watching the documentary series *Into the Unknown: Making Frozen II.* As a disclaimer, I'm not one of those mad Disney addicts who visit the theme park every year and celebrate every important milestone with a Mickey and Minnie flash mob. I've actually never been to either World or Land and hope to keep it that way. My children are eventually going to hate me for something; I might as well benefit. But I think anyone can appreciate the amount of work and talent that goes into making a movie like *Frozen,* and as a writer fascinated by creative processes, I found it illuminating to learn how the disparate elements of animation, music, and storyline were brought together into one grand symphony.

Beyond the fractals of technology and art, one thing I found especially interesting was Lee's energy—how calm and kind she seemed. When she was being interviewed, for example, she switched places with the interviewer so that she sat not behind her desk but on the other side. It was a humble gesture, I thought, something rarely seen in documentaries about Hollywood big shots. It was refreshing to watch a woman navigate such an enormous amount of work and responsibility and succeed at that level without the tough bitch armor so many other women feel forced to wear.

So the first thing I did after the end of the last episode was Google Lee's speeches, because that's what I do. I found a commencement address she had made in 2014 in which she told a very long personal story about her struggle with self-doubt, both while she was growing up and as an adult. The similarity between her trials and tribulations and those of the *Frozen* heroine, who struggles to reconcile her immense power with her lack of confidence, is hard to miss. Some people may have found the speech moving and very honest in this way, but to me—at the risk of completely alienating myself forever from the filmmaking set—it felt somewhat indulgent given the audience and the forum. After all, here was a room of students celebrating the major accomplishment of completing their degrees, and they were met in the moment by Lee's pain and suffering.

There is, however, an amazing moment at around the seven-minute mark that would have been stunning if it had been the first thing out of her mouth (and with a little Oratory Laboratory tinkering, of course). Lee said: "In film school, the first thing you learn is character. And you learn that insecure characters, characters who don't think they're good enough, are not very interesting. They're not inspiring and hopeful and nobody wants to watch them. Ouch. But the only characters worse than insecure characters are perfect characters. They are lifeless and boring and generic and they never feel authentic." She then explained—and I paraphrase, because it took her too long to get there—that the best characters, the ones with whom we identify, are flawed and unique.

That's it! I thought when I watched it. That's where her speech should have started. It's something we don't know. It's a personal story. But right away it gives her an entry point to a much more uplifting character to describe: the flawed, imperfect character with a lot to learn—a perfect mirror image of the newly graduated student. And she could have peppered this new narrative with stories of her personal struggles without having to divulge her life story tragedy by tragedy and in chronological order to get there. Unfortunately, having done just that, she'd painted herself as the very character she'd described as not thinking they were good enough and thus uninspiring. If she'd led with what she'd learned at film school and segued into learnings from Pixar's collaborative writing process and about how she came to understand the value of critique versus criticism, she could have used her life experiences to back up the themes, rather than leading with those experiences.

It's hard to know how much of a front seat to take in your own speech. You'll see politicians having to negotiate this dance often. When does the electorate become the main focus? When is the candidate expected to give something of themselves? Knowing where you belong in the narrative is important to establish early because it affects whether you go to your own recollections or go looking for data or other examples (such as stories of other characters from the recent past or rituals in other parts of the world) to back up your case. It will inform the type of stories you draw from and how you use them. We can't ever fall into the trap of being too self-involved; rather, we must counteract that by striving for human connection with the audience.

I understood that my client, Maggie, the museum founder, didn't want to talk about her breakdown, but the pages and pages of material she sent me on her career and the charitable organizations in which she'd been involved amounted to a resume and not much more. "Maggie," I told her, "I understand what you've done, but now I need to know why you did it." I wanted the emotional truth amid the factoids and laundry list of accomplishments. At my insistence she finally began to describe her early childhood and her family as the motivating factors for the path she took, and it was out of these anecdotes that we were able to create a couple of beautiful metaphors about the meaning of community engagement and sacrifice. She didn't have to be the main character, but she certainly deserved a supporting role.

PART TWO
The Material

4

The Interrogation

Beyond the Stuff You
Know You Know

As the speaker—and as the haver of thoughts, experiences, ideas, and knowledge—you step up to the job with a great deal of the material for your speech already right there in that brain of yours (and with some of it potentially in emails and documents an assistant compiled too). You may not have a clue what to do with that material, but there's no doubt it's up there. One of the things I suspect many people fear about speechwriting is what might happen if they try to put pen to paper. Specifically, what if nothing happens? But at some point you need to be able to articulate the early inklings you might have about the content without worrying about eloquence and impact. I can assure you that with permission to be spontaneous and erratic and to freely associate between things that don't even make sense, you'll find 70 percent of the substance of the speech in those pages of notes. A brain dump should be liberating, but you have to give yourself permission to be clumsy, clunky, and as incoherent as comes naturally—you're merely offloading at this point. My early notes are barely legible, let alone intelligible: missing words, sentences without endings, lots of bullet points, and questions to answer later.

You might choose to do this exercise with a notepad and pen, with your feet up on a sofa. You might prefer a quiet room and a glowing blank screen. When I have to go through this process for a personal assignment versus for someone else, I find using a pen is the only way to really allow those random connections to take shape. I find that if I type, I'm too easily able to delete an "incorrect" thought in an act of self-sabotage or self-consciousness. While writing this book I had a number of large legal pads on the desk around my computer and monitor as well as pages and pages of notes that I could tear out and move around as I worked through the initial thoughts of each chapter. It left very little space for much else on my desk, so most of my notes were stained with my morning almond butter, coffee, and my "speed salad dressing," which is always too tart. You could probably tell when I wrote which chapters by the types of food stains on my notes. Perhaps this detail is something I should have deleted.

When I work with a speaker the closest thing to a brain dump begins in the later stages of the Creative Kickoff and is followed up in a more cohesive formulation in the 20 Questions. The 20 Questions are the cornerstone of my creative methodology. Contrary to the children's game in which one person picks an animal, profession, or country and the other players ask yes-or-no questions, The Oratory Laboratory's 20 Questions are designed with the express intention of eliciting thoughtful, detailed, and highly specific answers. It's not hyperbole to say that the consistency with which I use this survey as an interviewing technique is the closest I ever come to anything religious. (Nathan and I are Jewish, but the Passover Haggadah he published espouses theories of alien invasion, includes an ode to Tupac, and describes Elijah as a heavy metal god, so there's that.)

I send the 20 Questions to every client, and though no two 20 Questions documents in my archives of hundreds upon hundreds are identical, each is crafted with the same objective in mind: to delve deeper into the themes and ideas that were surfaced during the Creative Kickoff and to un-cover the unexpected details, untold stories, imperfect opinions, and lesser-known facts that, based on my creative brief, I know will endow the narrative with texture, orig-inality, authenticity, and humanity. Why are there twenty, you ask? Because twenty is purposeful and intentional and it forces me to deploy each one with precision and care. No wasteful, lazy questions at The OL! Besides, what would you call a questionnaire of fewer than twenty items? The Questions? Some Questions? Your Questions? Far too ge-neric for my liking.

Speakers come to The Oratory Laboratory at different stages of preparedness—and that stage is often, though not always, determined by their eagerness to speak. They may have been invited to say something, feel obligated to do so, or have actively sought out the opportunity, and how they feel about it ranges from insecurity (*What the hell will I talk about?*) to overconfidence (*I know exactly what I want to say*) accordingly. No matter how certain a speaker might be about the point of view they want to share, what is certain is that no one arrives with a perfectly clear idea about how they're going to turn a single thought or even a few into a five-, ten-, or forty-minute speech. The 20 Questions get us most of the way there. They build on and interrogate much of what was brought up in the initial meeting, but their function hinges tightly on the kind of speech we're crafting.

If you were to examine the internal workings of The Oratory Laboratory, you'd see that the division between speeches about people and speeches about things is delineated at every level. I rarely have the same writer work across the two genres, and the writer training process is different for the two. I also insist that writers working on speeches about people wear only red to symbolize warmth and love and writers who work on speeches about things wear blue to denote blue-sky thinking. I'm completely joking about that last part, of course. Most notably, though, the lens through which the 20 Questions are composed is angled differently for each genre. One angle asks the speaker for deep, unrestrained introspection. The other asks the speaker for meticulous, granular detail.

When you're speaking about a person, it's not enough to prioritize that person as the main character in your narrative, as I explained in the previous chapter. You have to be really specific about what you say. Audiences at weddings and funerals want to laugh and cry at the things they know about their loved ones already and at things they are learning for the first time. But that doesn't mean they want to hear that the bride is into yoga and *The Bachelor*. Let's be honest: that pretty much describes every millennial city-dwelling female who got a job straight out of college. Instead, they want to know why she does it and what it says about her specifically. What makes her yoga practice different from the next person's? For example, does she sometimes skip the shower after? Does she look the wrong way in Warrior Two every time like I do? And why doesn't she watch the Kardashians or *Queer Eye* or the one where everyone wears bikinis and tries not to sleep with each other? These kinds of insights will shed light on something we perhaps didn't know and that cannot be said about anyone else. Given the repetitive rituals of weddings and bar mitzvahs and other rites of passage, the single most important objective should be to craft a speech that cannot be made about the next bride getting married in the venue next weekend.

When I was planning my own wedding, I received a request from a woman in New York who told me she had two weddings coming up and she had been asked to be the maid of honor at both. "Can you just write me a really generic template that I can use for both?" she asked me on an introductory call. "You know, it can just be really vague, we don't have to do the Creative Kickoff or the twenty questions or anything." I was incensed and vented to my sister that weekend that I'd been contacted by a total moron who thought she could somehow deliver the same speech about two different people without even doing an interview with me. Caroline agreed. Moron, indeed; what was she thinking? Weeks later, after Caroline delivered a lovely speech as my own star maid, she confessed that in an attempt to pull off a hilarious stunt she had enlisted the help of the moron to pretend on Caroline's behalf that she needed the speech. The goal was to get me to write a speech about myself that Caroline would give at the wedding and reveal as an Oratory Laboratory product. It would have been an ingenious plan were it not for the meticulous creative process that prevented its success.

When training new writers, we talk a lot about what makes

a smart question—the kind that leads to a truly unique speech—especially when it comes to speeches about people. The more specific we can be as interviewers, the better we set up the client for success. If we can paint a scenario for the speaker or focus their attention on a moment in time, it will be easier for them to answer that question. The 20 Questions are always customized according to whatever conversation took place in the Creative Call, but after twelve years I know which questions draw out the best information about people, so we also pull from a pool of evergreen content. For a wedding, a bar mitzvah, or a eulogy, for example, you might expect to receive questions such as:

> *Cast your mind back . . . Your daughter is fifteen; what's hanging on her bedroom walls?*
> *What is the one consistent piece of feedback on your son's school report card that always surprises you?*
> *What's the funniest thing your daughter did before the age of thirteen?*
> *It's Saturday at noon and you desperately need to find your mother—where do you go first?*

In Walter's case, the question about the bedroom walls prompted a very particular memory of a Madonna poster his daughter had stuck up on the wall behind her bed, which had ignited an almighty argument. It culminated in Walter storming into the bedroom and ripping the poster down. Walter was incensed by the Jean Paul Gaultier bra (such a heathen!) and found it highly inappropriate. His daughter felt her personal space was hers to decorate as she chose. She didn't speak to him for weeks. It was the perfect accompaniment to Walter's description of the fiercely opinionated and independent young woman she still was today. If we had simply asked him what his daughter was like as a teenager, he might never have recalled the poster at all and she would have sounded like every other teenage girl.

When it comes to a speech about things, typically addressing your peers and other professionals (rather than family and friends), the 20 Questions are much more fluid and reactive to the speaker and the topic. Having told you already that infusing personal experience into a speech requires a degree of objectivity in order to determine how much and when, I will say that this chapter is a caveat. Even if I'm working on a speech with a dental surgeon for, say, a roomful of medical professionals who are eager to hear the latest developments about a machine with lots of hyphens and numbers in its name and who are less interested in warmth and connection, I still try to create those human moments (though getting there can be like pulling teeth).

People don't call upon famous quotes because they enjoy memorizing words; they do it because they remember how the quote made them feel when they first heard it. TED's Chris Anderson says that, as a speaker, you're not trying to manipulate the audience. I agree, but you need to connect with them emotionally, and the line between the two is razor thin. There are few speeches I've written over the past twelve years in which at least wrestling with the idea of attaching something personal to a speaker's narrative—no matter how distantly they might want to position themselves from the narrative—has not been absolutely fundamental to the final outcome of the piece. As temporary as the entanglement might be and as indulgent as it may seem, getting intimate with your subject will always produce the most authentic ideas, even if the relationship between you and the subject is not explicit in the text. People talk about authenticity a lot, but without understanding its nuances. It's not just about being genuine; it's about bringing yourself to a narrative even when your role is not immediately evident. You don't have to be the hero of the speech to get personal.

Remember Sherri, the bikini-wearing astronaut who makes me cry? When we first worked with her on the planetarium speech, she had no clue what she wanted to talk about. When you're asked to speak at, say, a business conference, a fund-raiser, an opening, or a yearly meeting, you're typically given top billing because of something you know, something you've experienced, something you've done, or something you're going to do. But in Sherri's case, it was her entire resume itself that qualified her for that particular podium—her accomplishments as an engineer, her contributions as an astronaut trainer, and her work in designing the civilian extraterrestrial experience.

I was training a writer at the time, so I suggested she take the Creative Call and send me her suggestions for the 20 Questions. We knew from our initial exploration of the brief that the audience would be expecting to hear about her career in some respect, and given that it was a women-in-science award, they would probably be interested in her experience as a female aeronautical engineer. We also assumed they would be eager to hear insights about space travel. So we asked her plenty of questions about the things she knew and her area of expertise, because part of our job is to become an expert too. But it was a question about a memorable moment outside of her professional career that revealed the theme of the whole speech. Referring to her recent work in the private sector of space travel, we asked Sherri:

You are tasked with giving a group of humans what is sure to be one of the most memorable moments of their lives. What's a moment from your life on earth that was defining? First kiss? Childbirth? Graduating? Crashing a car? Seeing ET?

She replied:

I have a few defining moments: my wedding day, the birth of each daughter, visiting the Royal Observatory in Greenwich for the first time and being dumbstruck by the profoundness of that. Greenwich deserves some explanation—if you stop and think about it, there are shockingly few things that the world has "agreed to agree on." We don't agree on languages, calendars, spiritual beliefs, you name it. And yet somehow we all use the same defining coordinate system to describe our home planet: the equator, the poles, and the prime meridian. So I find personal magic in the crosshairs of the Airy telescope, which defined that coordinate system for all of humanity—and every engineering homework problem starts with drawing the coordinate systems of relevance. When I went to Greenwich I felt pure magic—a real connection to the power and promise of humanity through something as basic as the definition of our common coordinate system.

Bullseye! In that answer we understood that the speech wasn't about women in science. Or astronauts. It was about the possibility of unity in a galaxy far away and what that meant for unity here on earth. When we'd posed that question to her about a defining moment in her life, we'd had no idea if she would list her wedding and then stop there. It's lucky—both for her speech and for the opening line of this book—that she went beyond that.

We weren't looking to tell the story of the time she went to the observatory. We wanted to know and understand the world the way she did, and the only way to do this was to pepper her with questions about seemingly banal things. This is what I mean when I say that deep introspection will always uncover the most interesting and authentic material that becomes the building blocks of your narrative.

If you strip away the question we asked Sherri to its bare bones, what we were essentially doing was identifying an emotional truth in her professional life (that by designing the passenger experience in civilian spaceflight she would change people's lives) and asking her to find something that might mirror this inflection point in her personal life. We had no idea that the unforgettable moment would be so beautifully tied into her work and the very reason she was speaking. If she'd told us a whole other tale about, say, a Buddhist retreat during which she'd decided she'd never crush another spider, we would have used it to different effect or perhaps not bothered at all. Similarly, when we asked her our next question, we thought something bigger might come of it. As it transpired, her response made for a funny icebreaker at the top of the speech.

Do you have any recollection as to what or who triggered your fascination with space?

She answered:

> *My mom likes to say that when I was a baby she saw a head-line about a space mission and said to herself, "Oh, I hope she never does anything like THAT."*

Another handy strategy of interrogation is to investigate the personal experiences that directly conflict with the dominant theme, as in the case of George—a self-described bookworm who in his commencement address wanted to talk about how books motivated him, but for whom, as we soon discovered, a disastrous career in high school and college sports provided a far more interesting way to talk about motivation.

George had been on the original team of executives at one of the biggest tech companies before it started on a trajectory toward world domination, and in the years after he left that company, he decided to use his wealth, influence, and passion for reading to launch an educational nonprofit organization.

The first time we'd partnered with him had been a couple of years earlier, crafting a birthday speech for a family member. He'd invited fifteen friends and their children on an all-expenses-paid trip during which they'd not only stayed together in a world-class hotel but also enjoyed a daily itinerary of private tours and extreme sports activities in some of the most breathtaking locations in the world. No need to feel envious—my most recent milestone birthday party was a fictionalized Fred Savage Fan Club reunion at a hotel bar, ahead of which, and without my knowing, my husband created an online store of customized Fred Savage merchandise and invited all attendees to purchase and wear at least one piece. The logo on the hoodies, fanny packs, tees, and caps all sported an illustration of me and Fred designed using photos. And it was all doable in Manhattan, so really, no need to fly halfway across the world, you know?

This time, George had been invited to address graduating students at his mother's alma mater, and he wanted to talk about his mother's influence, bibliophilia, and "finding your fuel," as he put it in his email. I bristled a touch on reading this last item, on account of its corporate corniness, but I gave him the benefit of the doubt and assumed he'd let me reframe it. It was, after all, a commencement speech, so it was hardly surprising that he intended to imbue the speech with some kind of motivational jargon, but since he knew me already, I hoped he'd trust me to make good choices. "I've got a few ideas," he wrote, "but don't yet have a speech, and am very mindful of wanting to tie my own experiences together in a way that is genuinely helpful and inspirational to the graduates." Music to my ears. He understood his job as a commencement speaker, and in offering up these ideas, no matter how rudimentary in their development, he had given me a direction for the topics on which to probe him further.

Luckily, George knew what to expect from the 20 Questions. In my personal life I probably spend far too much effort trying to be nice when I'm asking people for things. My emails are far too long and elaborate. I chat up customer service people on the phone in an attempt to be charming. I like to be likable. But when it comes to the 20 Questions I don't care as much for niceties or deference. I will use every available opportunity to remind the speaker that if they don't make the effort in completing the 20 Questions—if they leave answers blank or give me halfhearted responses that came off a talking point drafted by an assistant—the mediocrity of the speech will be their burden to bear. I take very seriously the covenant made between speaker and writer. It is a collaboration in which I am a proxy only in the creative role. To return to our culinary metaphor, if you get me half the ingredients I asked for to make the curry, the chances are it will be tasteless. If you go in search of local ingredients from farmers' markets and specialty food stores, I can make the best damn curry the guests will have ever had. Which is more than I can say for my real curry. It's not good.

I already knew from our first collaboration that George had grown up with his nose in books, hiding in the fantasy section of the local library. So in this new batch of 20 Questions I asked him to recall the most embarrassing sports-related moment from high school. Assuming—correctly, as it turned out—that George wasn't exactly a jock, I was curious to hear about his shortcomings and pain points as well as his strengths.

Certain clients will often respond to the questions in which I play devil's advocate with an emphatic "This is irrelevant," which drives me bananas, quite honestly—if you ask someone for help and then tell them what they're doing isn't correct, why bother asking them at all? My father does this in restaurants—it's still his favorite way to embarrass me in my forties. He first asks the server if the bartender knows how to mix a "good" mojito. As if the server is going to say, "Well, actually, between you and me, Keith is really overpaid and underqualified." When the server replies yes, he orders it in a way that suggests he's doing the establishment a favor. Then when he is served the drink, he performs a long, drawn-out taste test, after which he inevitably snorts in disgust and mumbles about it being "fine." As if he has ever in his life mixed a cocktail successfully or has any idea what a "good" mojito is. When I'm told a question is irrelevant, I think about that mojito, dig my heels in further, and insist that it be answered. I told you, I take this very seriously.

Sure enough, George's answer provided the goods for which I was hoping. Baked into one of his delightfully long-winded and uncensored responses he offered up a story about a pair of cycling shorts his mother had bought him at graduation. (Of course he loved cycling. It made perfect sense—the nerdy kid who liked to lose himself in adventures felt most comfortable on a journey designed for one.) Those cycling shorts became a delightful opener for the speech and a setup to one of the themes that came later:

> *Before I say anything else, I want to give you all [graduates] a huge round of applause and I encourage you to join me. This is a big moment for you. I hope you all feel incredibly proud of yourselves for getting here. I graduated long enough ago that it's all a little hazy now. But I do remember that to mark the occasion, shortly afterward my mother sent me a very special gift.*
>
> *A pair of cycling shorts.*
>
> *Yes, cycling shorts. Now, I don't have to tell you that there's nothing particularly cool about cycling shorts, and these ones didn't even have a swoosh or a hip design to make me look a pro; they were from L.L.Bean. Good old L.L.Bean—they do make one helluva pair of spandex shorts. What was especially remarkable about them was that they were khaki, so really it looked like I wasn't wearing any cycling shorts at all. I never thought I'd actually long for that signature L.L.Bean red plaid.*

But these cycling shorts really were special. Because when I put them on it was like stepping into the closet that would lead me to Narnia. Right in that very moment I was overcome by a sense of adventure and curiosity. All I wanted to do was go. And when I tell you that I jumped on my bike almost immediately, I'm only exaggerating in that I left time to call my mom and thank her for picking out such a great color before setting off on an epic two-hundred-mile ride from Boston to Maine without a plan or a clue of how to actually get there.

My mother's influence on me stretches way beyond spandex. She'll be pleased to hear that; she's actually here today—Hi, Mom! She is the one who always taught me to just do the thing that made sense to me in the moment. She practiced that philosophy herself, and as a kid, it rubbed off on me like the grease from my bike chain . . .

That's why I'm here today. To celebrate you for how far that [name of college] spirit has brought you already, and to tell you that your course from here depends on nothing but your ability to keep saying to yourself, "To hell with it, this feels right—just do it."

One question about being a nerd, and the whole speech opened up.

Just the other day, a major stakeholder at Citi told me that answering my questions felt like sitting in the analyst's chair. I used to talk about my interview process as imitating therapy long before I even really knew what that meant. Thank God I was right. (Although now I have a therapist's bill, which isn't so great.) The process is intensely personal and can be uncomfortable, but just as in therapy, if you don't go through the discomfort, then you don't make progress. When you're given the space to pour your heart out and try to articulate your most emotionally indulgent thoughts and feelings, the more interesting, useful stuff inevitably emerges when you're enticed to go a layer deeper. I listened to a podcast the other day where the producer said to his guests, "Tell me the story and I'll poke you along the way." I thought, *Yes! It's all about poking in the right direction.* We walk around with memories, theories, wisdom, experiences, anecdotes, beliefs, and opinions that, because we assume they are unimportant, we keep bottled up, until one day someone asks the right question and they all just come tumbling out.

The question you might well be asking, however, is, what if you're that someone? How does one psychoanalyze oneself? (Wouldn't that be something.) It would be disingenuous of me to tell you there is any prescribed quiz one could apply to all speeches. But if you've done the work of establishing some version of a brief based on the initial questions of where, why, and who, then you already have a rubric through which to evaluate your material. When you pull up all the notes you've made and review what you set out to do for both yourself and your audience, ask yourself whether you're succeeding in this with the material from your brain dump. Are there enough intimate confessions to satisfy the audience? Is there shock and awe? Are you providing lessons that can be carried into work the next day? Is there an aspirational message of empowerment? Perhaps the audience is looking for intellectual insights so as to come away feeling that they're better armed for the next political debate at the family Thanksgiving table.

They might want to feel like they belong. Do they want leadership or an ally? In short, what is missing?

I may not be able to tell you the exact and perfect questions to ask yourself, but I can offer you this story as a way to think about the process of interrogating your own ideas in order to access deeper and richer material.

There was a time not long ago when, every day, I—along with millions of parents the world over—had to stop what I was doing to upload my second grader's writing exercises to her remote schooling app. In our case it was Google Classroom. I knew I was meant to just take a picture and upload the file and let the teachers deal with it. And God, I wanted so badly to do only that—I mean, when I was younger I wanted to be a lawyer, a pilot, and an actress, but never a teacher. And yet the writer in me couldn't resist reading her work and trying to help her improve on her answers. She had provided the fastest, most economical answers every time. If the question was "What does the character's superpower show about her?" she'd answer, "That she was strong." The irony is that out in the street she stops every single person who crosses her path with a question about their dog or their friend or the reason they chose the pink hair dye and why they picked that tattoo and that body part. My favorite is when she asks couples if they live together.

So I would sit with her and ask her to put the paper down and just chat with me for a moment. I recited the answer she gave me and then I subjected her to the same scrutiny by asking her the most basic questions: Why did she answer that way? Why does she think the character in her book did what she did? That tiny "why" was all it took to travel deeper into her small but perfect well of experience and understanding.

What if it's just as simple as recalling that childish curiosity we all have within us? Of taking each piece of material, every story and data point we think is the pinnacle of our expertise, and daring to ask: *Why? Why do I think this? How do I know it's true? What is my experience of it? What don't I know because I know this?*

I don't always get what I need from the 20 Questions. Some people who aren't invested in the process are only capable of one-word answers. It's disheartening. In this case I go back with Four More selected from the four answers in the initial twenty that I feel I can crack open further, and I ask these childish questions. Give me more detail, I implore. But I beg of you, don't censor yourself yet. You never know where you might find those cycling shorts.

5

The Investigation

The Research That Enriches Your Narrative

I remember reading a riveting article in *New York Magazine* once about the famed private eye Marie Schembri. As an investigator in the pre-internet age, she would deck herself out in disguises of all varieties to stake out her targets. She wore wigs, popped bubblegum, and adopted fake tics, all to get close to the suspicious party she was investigating without blowing her cover. Nowadays, she says, she can do all her research on stalkers or unfaithful spouses from her home computer. She sifts through archives, records, and camera footage, allowing her curiosity to lead her down rabbit holes in search of a phony account or an undisclosed third home. It's not so unlike what I find myself doing on any given day when I'm gathering material for a speech. I wonder if Schembri still wears the wigs and costumes; I know I do.

Now, let me clarify—I don't stalk my clients in the way Schembri does, acquiring personal information and data from public records. But I do share her knack for taking a kernel of information, whether an offhand remark or reference, and then digging up as much on it as I can. And it is without a doubt my favorite stage of the process. It's fun to fantasize about sleuthing à la Schembri or some glamorous MI5 operative. When I plugged Nathan's number into my phone years ago, I made his contact name NATO because I'd heard his stepmother shout to him that way in her thick Israeli accent, and I confess I sometimes get a kick out of the fact that when I tell Siri to call NATO, anyone overhearing this might actually think I'm dialing into some covert military operation. (I said "might.")

The very first speech I ever wrote for anyone under the auspices of The Oratory Laboratory was a toast a J.Crew stylist would be making at her brother's fortieth birthday party. She'd told us he'd gone back to work at the family apple orchard after a ten-year stint making documentaries and that, inexplicably, he'd decided to plan a party for himself in July even though the anniversary of his birth wasn't until October. She guessed he'd wanted a summer outdoor bash and expected more of his friends to turn up in July. With only forty-nine hours to turn it around, without even having spoken to her on the phone and just a limited amount of information from an early iteration of our questionnaire, I looked at what I had and, curious to know more about her brother, searched his name and the word "apples" and was quickly directed to the website of the family farm. I learned about what apples grew there and all kinds of exciting agricultural information. I always say the only thing I'm an expert on is writing speeches, but I know a little about a lot thanks to this job. What I also discovered was that October was when the farm held its Harvest Festival. Now, that may sound obvious to you, but at the age of twenty-eight, this Londoner-turned–New Yorker wasn't exactly tuned in to the *Farmer's Almanac,* so it was a surprise to me—and it turned into a funny way to open the toast.

> *I have to say I don't know many others who would sacrifice the final three months of their thirties just so as they can make it to Harvest Festival. But such is Todd's dedication to his fruit that it will be only his apples who celebrate their maturity in October.*

Dana was tickled that we'd bothered to investigate her brother's life in that way and make that connection, and I made a mental note that stalking people online was both creepy and necessary.

How can I write a speech about something if I don't really know about it or own the experience? Most people who find out what I do can't reconcile this point with their misconceived notion of authenticity. The answer, of course, is that I have to be incredibly curious, I have to listen hard, and I have to be open to learning a lot that maybe isn't relevant at the end of the day. Often I start by knowing nothing about the subject; if I already have some understanding of it, I try to become more of an expert. As I go in search of the connective tissue that makes a speaker's material more compelling for the audience, I also have to grill the client on everything I think they can offer that's related to the subject matter—what they know, what they think about it, what experience has led them to this point of view—so that I know what to look for when I go off and read about the subject alone. When Marie Schembri is hired by the wife of a cheating husband to go through his cellphone log, she's not looking at every strange phone number that doesn't belong to her client. That would be time-consuming and futile. Instead, she's looking for the calls he made to her, specifically those that took place midweek at around 6:00 p.m. to say he'd be late home from the office, because right before or after that is the phone call to the significant "other."

Please understand, my modus operandi does not require that I go looking for dirt on anyone. Most clients are surprisingly forthcoming when it comes to confessions of mistakes made, soured relationships, and infidelity. Although I do recall a time one of my writers, suspecting she recognized the name and face of a client, Googled him and discovered to our astonishment that he had indeed featured in a true-crime reality show after his ex-wife had put a hit out on him. But like Schembri, when it comes to imagining how to make the information I have work harder, I too have to go through the proverbial phone log on the hunt for those juicy leads. There are many advantages to being curious and asking questions that go beyond what the speaker knows or at least provides, the first being that it helps me uncover clever-sounding ways to support the talking points and flesh out the arguments with more substantive evidence.

This was precisely the need with a big speech like Charlie's, for example. She had her own personal experiences as an actor in pornography to give her talking points credibility and create a human connection with the audience, but she was addressing an academic audience with a thirst for learning. We needed to become historians, anthropologists, and sociologists in a matter of weeks in order to educate them as well as entertain.

Nathan's immensely generous gesture of covering the

IMDB and YouTube portion of the research sent me on a more scholarly route. I started on Wikipedia (I said "started"—calm down) because I was curious how the internet and its users defined "pornography" and what they considered its essential history. But I also interviewed two professors of gender studies I knew well, and read a lot of essays about turn-of-the-century pornography and pro-sex feminism. One of the most fascinating moments of learning for me was the comparison of two definitions, which made it into the speech like this:

> So, here we are: you all watch porn, you maybe even go onto bondage sites, perhaps you watch it with your lover, but you're not going to talk about it at a party.
>
> Why?
>
> Let's all get on the same page about what the word means. Before I read the definition from dictionary.com, allow me to read another. This is the definition of murder: "Murder: The killing of another human being under conditions specifically covered in law."
>
> All right. Sounds pretty bad. Maybe illegal, but, you know, no judgment. Just objective fact.
>
> Keep that in mind as I read the definition of pornography: "Pornography: Obscene writings, drawings, photographs, or the like, especially those having little or no artistic merit."
>
> I mean, come on. Does that sound a little judgy to anyone else? "Obscene writings, drawings, photographs, or the like, especially those having little or no artistic merit."
>
> "The like"? "Little or no artistic merit"? Those folks at dictionary.com need to lighten up.

Before You Say Anything

*I think that says a lot about the way society has evolved
in its attitude toward crimes and acts of immorality.*

The result of all this research was that after the shock of
the double anal line, what followed was an elaborate discourse about the history of sex and commerce, the evolution
of social mores, and the nature of curiosity. Apparently curiosity can lead you to a career in speechwriting or a career in
pornography. I need to think about where I went wrong . . .

I get such a thrill when I learn on the job myself and a little
piece of my own mind is opened and shown a new perspective. I want to tell someone about it immediately, and usually that someone is Nathan at the end of the day, when he
makes the mistake of asking how my day went. On a research
day, he doesn't often get a word in edgewise.

A research day for me comprises the type of activity for
which in any typical job you'd be fired. It's the day—or sometimes more—that I spend following clickbait links and You-
Tube algorithms, stalking people's LinkedIn profiles, and
plumbing the depths of the web. It's very freeing when you
assign purpose to a behavior usually met with shame and disapproval. I scour news. I read all kinds of essays and studies.
I call upon books I've read or podcasts I've listened to, documentaries I've seen. When I'm working on a speech, I have
my radar switched on to pick up any frequency that might
turn up something of interest. You just never know where
you're going to find the treasure—in an episode of *Freako-
nomics* or in the comments of a Subreddit.

But building evidence and the substance of your central argument is only one reason to put your notes aside and spend

a day or two with your detective goggles on. Interrogation of what you know can offer up snippets that support your subject and make you sound smarter and more learned than you already are. Like the moment in which I discovered while writing a keynote on gender equality that the famous James Brown song "It's a Man's, Man's, Man's World" was written by a woman. What a brilliant aha moment that was! Of course, I had to check that I wasn't the last to know this. What may be an aha moment for me is very possibly a "yeah, duh" moment for someone else. But I surveyed some clued-in people whose cultural intelligence I trust deeply and none of them had known either. Sung by a man, the song was like a punch to the gut, but written by a woman, it stung.

Sometimes a day of exploration and curiosity even reveals the core message itself. But where do you even start researching if you're standing in the wilderness with only a vague sense of the direction your speech might take? I have found the setting in which the speech will be delivered is a great point from which to jump into research, especially if it's a noteworthy venue. When Goldie told me she was speaking at Sing Sing prison, I knew that would be where I started my research.

Goldie is a confident and driven creative from Brooklyn, and her credentials as an up-and-comer in the music industry and a community leader earned her an invitation from TEDx Sing Sing to come and speak. The hosts were impressed by the work she'd done in creating a studio space for young people of color called 24Ours. The name was a nod to the sense of belonging she hoped to create for stylists, photographers, musicians, and other creatives, who could pay a nominal fee for access to all the equipment that would usually cost a small fortune in studios where the general attitude was less than welcoming to her diverse crew of friends. At Sing Sing she'd be expected to speak on a theme put forward by the host: "Redefining What Matters," which I defined as "What Matters to You?"

For Goldie, a young woman whose father and brother had both served time in prison, the location carried implications beyond the geographical site. And I recognized that I knew little about the history and reputation of Sing Sing beyond what I'd watched in the movies. To my great satisfaction I stumbled very quickly upon a perfect connection between the name of the prison and how Goldie had described the intention behind 24Ours as building a network:

Stone upon stone.

I've thought about that a lot. It's the act of building something. One stone, upon another stone, upon another stone, until, in this case, you build a six-story maximum-security prison.

You know the other thing we build? We build a life. Or at least we try.

And when we talk about building a life, it's a vertical trajectory as well. People say they want upward mobility. They want to climb the ladder. Move up in the world. Raise their status. When we talk about ambition, we're reaching for the stars. When we start a business as an entrepreneur, we have to build from the ground up, scale up, setting your sights high, aiming for the top.

Success requires growth. It seems like up is the only direction we can go.

It's a lot of pressure.

The Investigation

I think of my family now: my dad in his jumpsuit, my mother in her dry cleaner job, feeling like she kind of lost her crown, my brother who got out of prison this year, and I wonder:
What if success wasn't just about building up?
What if it was about building out *instead?*

Building out was defined as investing in, enriching, and advancing communities instead of just individuals. Creating a socialist-capitalist utopia, if you will. If you can't dream in a speech, where can you?

Metaphor and analogy are such powerful and effective ways to engage an audience and draw them into your argument, and I lean on them just as heavily for speeches about people at funerals, weddings, and other milestone events. The springboard that propels me in the right direction to find them is almost always buried in the personal details.

For example, when Alex called me from his apartment in Brooklyn, he did so with a lot at stake. He would be speaking at his brother's wedding in their Southwestern hometown, and it had only been two years since their father's death, so his role had added import. He wanted to celebrate his brother, but he also wanted to acknowledge their absent father's impact on their lives, and fill his shoes in this important moment. Alex was charming and incredibly articulate. He talked about how, growing up, the two brothers had fought, but as his mother put it, "Alex always fought with words." Such was the emotional block with trying to write this speech, however, that he'd come to me for help. Alex confessed that he had always been regarded by his archetypical alpha-male brother and his friends as "a bit of a pussy" and that his homosexuality was generally glossed over by the family. He had a boyfriend in the East Coast city where he now lived, but no one knew. I could tell that, while still capturing the tone of a best man roast, Alex would appreciate a considered approach to the language and use of rhetorical devices.

One insight I highlighted in the answers to his 20 Questions was that his brother had an extensive collection of hats. That seemed excessive and therefore significant. What did that say about the brother? It wasn't that he was bald—that was of course my first question.

A few Google searches soon turned up an old piece of branded video content made by the very company whose stores the groom regularly visited for his favorite accessory. The tagline of the ad was: "Times Change, Traditions Don't." After absorbing all the stories Alex had told me about his father and his brother and the rituals they shared over the course of their lives, I realized that the collection of hats had offered up a perfect metaphor. Though it had kicked off the speech as a joke it suddenly carried so much more weight. It was a perfect way for Alex to describe his brother, how he had grown out of his high-wire antics, and how the memory of their father would live on.

These kinds of metaphors are all around us if we're curious enough to look. I cast a magnifying glass over all of the information shared with me, scouring the stories for mention of hobbies, brand names, organizations, people, jobs, countries, and other things that might produce riches.

I wasn't expecting a powerful real estate tycoon, for example, to take me on a journey back to the 1980s and Mr.

Miyagi. I'm a huge fan of 1980s teen movies. Nathan says he fell in love with the way I quoted John Hughes's entire oeuvre more than any of my other, many, redeeming qualities. Remember the Fred Savage Fan Club birthday party he threw for me? Well, four years prior, for my ninth birthday (remember, I was born on February 29 in a leap year), he rented out a movie theater in Brooklyn, and all my friends came to eat, drink, and watch *The Breakfast Club*. Man, I was so emotional that night, mouthing the words to Judd Nelson's monologue. I felt like my friends probably finally understood who I really was.

So: real estate, Mr. Miyagi . . . yes. I'd already worked with Eli on a birthday speech a year prior, so when he was invited by a speakers' forum to deliver a keynote about his fifty-year vision for the skyline of a fast-growing North American city, he called me. As one of that city's biggest developers, Eli already had very particular ideas about what he wanted to say, so our initial conversation was very productive. I crafted the 20 Questions with the goal of establishing a personal connection to these thoughts and to the profession to which he had dedicated his life. In one of the answers he mentioned having a bonsai tree as a kid. We had briefly discussed Eli's fascination with form and function and how those qualities combined provided the key to enduring infrastructure and the growth of a city. Knowing only what my *Karate Kid* education had taught me about bonsai trees, I decided to do a little research. My first mistake, as it turned out, was thinking that a bonsai was a species of small tree. Within minutes I had rooted out the correct definition. (Pun most definitely intentional.) In Japanese, *bonsai* means "dish tree."

In other words, a tree grown in a dish. On further reading I learned that bonsai trees were cultivated from cuttings of much larger trees that were constrained by encasements to limit their growth, thus making them miniature. A miniature tree one could keep at home. Function and form. It couldn't have been a more perfect example of his thesis statement. So the opening and setup of the speech was a very nostalgic and self-deprecating story of a teenager in the 1980s whose best friend was a bonsai tree and who grew into a developer obsessed by the idea of design and beauty. And I was able to use what I knew about the setting and cultural moment to further imbue the introduction with topical significance.

Before we think about where we might be in fifty years, I first want to take you back to 1985. Margaret Atwood had just written The Handmaid's Tale. *Back to the* Future *and* Karate Kid *had hit the silver screen. And the Maple Leafs were still terrible.*

I was fourteen, and while other kids were obsessed with Doc's time machine, I was captivated by something else: a bonsai tree. Maybe Mr. Miyagi was to blame—I can't remember—but whatever inspired me to purchase this tiny tree, I can tell you that it captured my imagination in a way no movie could. To me the beauty of this tree was magical. It was so delicate, yet so strong and defined in its essence. This was no regular houseplant. And to keep it alive I spent a lot of time caring for it. Pruning it first to determine its overall shape and then to maintain its structure. I wanted to make sure I nurtured and maintained its timeless beauty and respected its unique design.

I know what you're all thinking. Did this guy have any friends or what? I had a few, I think. . . .

But here's the thing you might not know about bonsai trees. Bonsai literally means "dish tree" in Japanese, or a tree that is grown in a shallow container. It is not a type or a species, but merely a tiny replica, grown in captivity by humans using leaves and branches from its parent or host. We don't mess with its DNA, but we give it parameters to limit its size and growth. In other words, we engineer its natural growth. At fourteen, the discovery of this organic marvel marked an important moment in my life. Because it made me look at the things around me and notice how often beauty and function coexist. It instilled in me a profound fascination and curiosity for how we design the things around us and how by paying attention to the smallest details they can endure. You might say that years before I had an iPhone, that bonsai tree was the first really beautifully designed thing I owned.

The bonsai tree became the framework for a speech about form and function, the central theme to Eli's vision of how the city's developers should think about building into the future. Eli believed that in order to plan the kind of city that might rival Paris or Tokyo, one had to think about enduring beauty rather than the immediate opportunity. He was certain his hometown was capable of becoming such a metropolis. And by the time I'd finished the speech I was convinced too. There have been so many reasons in the past few years to wonder about leaving the States; at least now I know where I would go if I did. At the end Eli was able to return to the tiny tree to conclude his thoughts.

Before You Say Anything

Like a tiny bonsai tree that is so often overlooked, our time-less and enduring beauty should never be underestimated.

There is of course such a thing as bad research. And bad research leads to bad speeches. Bad research is lazy research. It's quoting data that everyone's heard before, such as the fact that women earn 82 cents for every dollar that men make, without presenting a fresh take on what that wage gap might actually imply about the value of our work or what we women could be doing with the 18 cents' worth of time that's unpaid. Like letting it accrue and then booking a spa retreat right in middle of the busiest week. Lazy research is quoting Gandhi when you're making a speech about electric cars or talking about Frida Kahlo when you're making a speech at your best friend's wedding. The only reason to mention Kahlo would be because you'd made a joke about the bride's monobrow, and the only reason you'd do that is if she had a bloody good sense of humor about it and had long since either done something to divide them into two or the monobrow had become the latest cause célèbre within the world of hipster beauty.

I've argued with clients about overused and clichéd poetry so many times I could write a poem about it. An original one at that! No one is going to think you're smart because you used an excerpt from *Don Quixote* or quoted Maya Angelou unless the reason you've done so is smart in itself. I don't think there's anything wrong with using a quote, and I understand that Maya Angelou can say things better than most of us, but when I do it, I make sure to take the quotes from people who feature in or are some unexpected but inarguable way associated with the story I'm telling. Like the way I used Winston Churchill at the beginning of this book!

For example, in a bat mitzvah speech, an excited mother quoted the character Anna—the ginger-haired ditzy-but-brave sister to *Frozen*'s ice queen, Elsa—telling the crowd gathered in the temple that she was pretty sure she was elated rather than gassy. Why? Not because I was obsessed with Jennifer Lee at the time of writing the speech, I swear! Because her daughter was obsessed with *Frozen* and had performed it just recently onstage. In a maid of honor's speech delivered to her Australian Chinese best friend in Sydney, the "maid" (I wish we could change these labels; it's so Gilead) acknowledged that the new husband referred to her as "June's suspiciously Caucasian sister." So we found a quote in Chinese—verified and spelled correctly, of course—from a well-known book whose translation the two friends had loved reading together. It spoke to the theme of sisterhood (from which I would usually run a mile) and satisfied a desire the client had expressed in the Creative Kickoff to say something in Chinese.

I may be asking a lot. When I train writers, I find it hard to pinpoint exactly how I know where the good quotes are hiding and what kind of material to mine further. It's so intuitive. What I identify as being worthy of closer inspection is not necessarily something someone else would even notice, and when I find something that piques my curiosity, I'm a bit like a dog with a bone. I skipped this part of my bio until now, but before I climbed aboard Nathan's family's minivan and traveled upstate, where my fate as a speechwriter would be sealed, I had rather fancied turning my attention to investigative writing for publications like *The Atlantic* and

The New Yorker. I'd done some feature reporting and relished the act of digging into a subject, uncovering everything there was to know about it, and then turning the pieces into a story. I'm no Jodi Kantor, nor am I a spy or a detective, but the research phase of my process most definitely scratches the itch. I may not be able to pass on intuition, but at the very least I can hope to make you itchy and then scratch that itch for you. Doesn't that sound lovely?

PART THREE
The Design

6

The "Crazy Wall"

Finding Unexpected
Connections in the Material

Not so long ago, an extremely upscale event planning company in New York that often sent their wedding clients my way asked if I'd be interested in collaborating with a different kind of client. They'd been hired by the host of one of America's biggest sporting events and were organizing the opening-night party. They asked me if I could work with the emcee to script his remarks. The speaker, it transpired, used to play for the host team and was slowly rising again from the ashes of a particularly controversial fall from grace. From the little I could gather on the initial call with the producer, the player was indebted to his former team's owner—the evening's host—and so made the perfect candidate for genuflection and flattery between entertainment segments.

Now, I love the US Open, I enjoy a good ice hockey brawl, and I'm really excited about the US women's soccer team—it's good football and their captains make great speeches. But even as I approach two decades stateside, when I think about baseball, American football, and basketball I go straight to jumbotrons, hot dogs, and brain damage. In fact, until I watched a Netflix docuseries about Michael Jordan, all I knew of the Chicago Bulls was the logo on a cap I got when I was seventeen, because you had to have a Bulls cap in the 1990s. At the time of this engagement, my reference points for the NFL were Tom Brady and the movie *Ace Ventura*. Laces out!

This meant that researching the speaker and the sport was both eye-opening and sobering. I love my work for so many reasons, but one I cherish in particular is that it forces me to check my biases. Being judgmental might be human (and perhaps in my case genetic), but when it comes to telling a story it can only be a barrier. The stories I read online about his scandal were a chorus of disgust and disapproval. He'd been canceled for something he'd done way before cancel culture became a thing, but when I paid closer attention to the quieter voices in his defense, I was so glad to have had the excuse to really understand all sides of the argument and see all the angles. I think a lot of people know what that feels like today.

When we finally spoke, the player was very charming and funny. He spoke with ease about his experience on the team and it would have felt like an honest dialogue were it not for the silent but breathy presence of the team's PR manager on a third line, ensuring we never strayed too far from their boilerplate talking points. After the call I didn't speak to him again, and I was cut out of the revision process while they peppered it with plenty of "on-message" jargon and gratuitous flattery. They were kind enough to send me an edited draft so I could see just how devoid of personality it had become, but I was pleased to see that at the very least they'd left in the setup I'd crafted. I'd been able to create a very satisfying metaphor by drawing a parallel between the host owner's former career as an entrepreneur and his foundation's work in the underserved communities of his team's home turf. If we pretend he was Victor Mills, who created Pampers, and then we pretend that between tending to his cactus garden and going on cruises Victor Mills later established a charity for refugee resettlement—which, as far as I know, he didn't—the big takeaway was that Victor "doesn't just protect the bottoms of children of America, he's protecting the futures of families all over the world." Or something to that effect. Maybe without bottoms.

At a certain point you have to stop gathering material and start thinking about what the hell to do with it all. This is where the plan to organize the cluttered and chaotic attic in your mind starts to take shape and you begin to make choices about where to store the turpentine in relation to that bag of rubber body parts you used with that improv troupe. In the food analogy it's where you lay out the ingredients you have on hand and reflect on the different ways you could use the butter, the olives, and the ketchup. Yuck. Sorry. But let's stick with the sleuthing theme because for this, you'll definitely want to keep your Inspector Gadget (or Burberry) trench on.

I find it's easier to sketch a narrative arc—that is, the key beats of a speech from start to finish—if I can shake free from the sequential order of things and undo the chronology by which I came upon the information. The goal is to try to extract all the pieces from each other, jumble them up as if they were tiles in a game of Scrabble, and then find a more unusual way to make sense of it all. Over the years I've changed my outlining practices more often than I changed the outline of this book. Which is a lot—I went through at least twelve outlines and twice as many ridiculous titles. It's hard even for me to see the forest for the trees when I work on my own. And that's how I ended up with what I call the Crazy Wall. The Crazy Wall is a physical board or a screen on which I randomly place the pieces of material and information I've been gathering in preparation to write the speech. It is a nod to the fact that there is no correct way to structure and outline a speech. There's just how you get from the beginning to the end along the most original path possible. As a strategy, the Crazy Wall is both empirical and imaginative—if you're a creative type, you should jump for joy, and if you're an organizer and planner, there is reason to be excited too. The Crazy Wall is where these two qualities converge.

If you somehow didn't get sucked into the Showtime cult hit *Homeland,* there was an unforgettable scene in which the inscrutable genius of the heroine, CIA agent Carrie Mathison, is revealed in its full glory in the form of a wall-to-wall display of clues and evidence linking random terrorists to international organizations. Every overlapping map, photograph, transcript, and bank statement is color-coded, and the totality spreads like a rainbow from one side of the room to the other. It echoes the pinboard of red strings that connect murder suspects to victims in classic cop thrillers. The Oratory Laboratory version of the Crazy Wall, on the other hand, connects the various pieces of material gathered by researching and dialoguing with the client. And while it rarely leads to a murder conviction, it does help you figure out how to share your convictions.

On my wall I like to break the pieces apart and categorize

them, for two reasons: one is to isolate them so as to identify unlikely patterns and surprising connections, and the second is to ensure a balance of all the elements as I begin to weave them together. The most common titles I use to arrange the material are Anecdotes, Data, and Truths. More on those later. If you see you only have one data point, you're then able to ask yourself, *Do I need more or is that okay?* Or perhaps, simply, *I wonder what a data point might look like in this speech about my husband.*

Data is exactly what it says on the label. For example, 80 percent of people feel unfulfilled at work. (Depressing but true.) Data can work very hard for your point in the right type of speech, especially if the numbers are controversial and unexpected. A best man speech is unlikely to contain data, unless for comedy. A keynote might have more.

Truths are what they say on the label too—which I know is a contentious point these days. Examples of a truth might be that stock market fluctuations are making investors uncomfortable. Carbon emissions are increasing. Nathan does a hell of a good job of getting into a car in mime.

Anecdotes are harder to define in a tidy paragraph, so I've dedicated an entire chapter to that later.

These categories are fluid; the material doesn't always neatly fit into such stringent parameters. But whatever buckets you create, the aim is to take material from each of them to build a central argument, or The Point. The Point (of which there may be more than one if you are talking about a friend or delivering a speech with action items) drives the narrative, and it is around this that all the other material coalesces. It is the central message, the argument, whatever you want to call it.

As I warned you, it's hardly the stuff of a suspense thriller, but the purpose of the Crazy Wall is to answer the same burning question every detective wants to answer: How does all this fit together? The fun is that where a detective would surely be the one who ended up in the slammer if they were to get "creative" with the answer to that question, there is no hard-and-fast conclusion you have to draw when it comes to crafting a speech. It has to be logical and easy to follow for those listening, but how you weave together your narrative is entirely up to you. The Crazy Wall is simply a conduit to the most exciting and original way.

I oscillate between three versions of the Crazy Wall, depending almost entirely on my energy and location. The most low-tech but highly caffeinated version of the Crazy Wall is a giant whiteboard covered in multicolored notecards, pins, and Post-it notes. On each notecard are keywords that represent each of the individual pieces of information and anecdotes I've gathered, boiled down so as to be identifiable at a glance. When I'm dealing with a big forty-minute keynote and I've got stats and information, press releases, research, answers to the 20 Questions, and more to wrangle, standing up and standing back can really help. I'm drawn to this tangible version when I'm alert, I'm plugged into a good Spotify playlist, and I have enough space to dance and pace. It's the closest to Carrie Mathison I have much chance of becoming, though I should make clear that the "crazy" aspect of the Crazy Wall does not in any way relate to anyone's mental stability. It's crazy simply because, compared to the impossibly precise outcome that is the speech, this moment is chaotic. And because if you were to tell anyone who saw you swaying in front of it that it's how you're writing your speech, they'd most likely think it was at least a quirky if not crazy way to go about it.

If getting amped up on coffee and Burna Boy is not for you, there's always tea and Yo-Yo Ma to accompany a more sedentary version, which is less wall but no less crazy. For speeches in which the caseload is much smaller, I sometimes print out all the documents I have, find a comfortable sitting or lounging position, and get to work with a highlighter and pen. Since I've been doing this for a long time, I find the connections come very naturally and I don't always need to see the pieces separately. I use my highlighter to distinguish between content I want to use and anything uninteresting or generic, and I use my pen to draw arrows, asterisks, under-lines, and other traditional editing shorthand, not to edit but to categorize and connect the different pieces.

Alternatively, I defer to the Crazy Screen, but this is really effective only if you have more than one monitor. Wherever I find myself working, I try to always have a second screen so I can open multiple windows and see them all together. On MacBooks you also have the option of swiping between desktops, and I do sometimes create my draft document on a second desktop so as not to be distracted by my emails. I know I could just close the email down, but that would be sensible and not at all crazy, now, wouldn't it?

When using this third, on-screen option for the Crazy Wall, I keep all the documents containing the original content open. I have a document named "Material," a document named "Outline," and a window open for further research. I also at some point open a document named "Draft." These documents are no more kempt than the wall of notecards or the scribbled-upon, well-thumbed documents. In the digital version the handwritten scrawl and stacks of jumbled pages are replaced by overlapping windows, each covered in caps, highlights, font variations, underlined sentences, comments, and replies to my own comments.

In whatever form feels most natural to you, the Crazy Wall is where you'll work out your outline. But even before that, it can actually help shape and define the specific subject—The Point—of your speech if you still don't know what it is. A lot of my clients have a sense of what that might be when they come to me, but for those who are still grappling with an unspecific and flexible invitation to "say something" about a general topic, I find the Crazy Wall can be a guiding light. In fact, a star was at the center of a thesis statement I cracked after a week spent staring at the Crazy Wall.

The client, we'll call her Mimi, was asked to make a speech at a women's networking event. The party was to be hosted by the American branch of a global company acclaimed for its equitable hiring practices and positive female-centric culture. Seemingly the event coordinator had been seduced by Mimi's wide-ranging experience, which spanned banking, the nonprofit sector, the travel industry, and entrepreneurship, but she had given Mimi no specific recommendation or preference as to the substance or specific angle of her speech. Mimi, someone I respected enormously for her achievements and ideas, was treading water in a vast ocean of possibilities with no sign of land in sight. She knew she wanted to and was expected to talk about gender equity, a topic so broad that people have written countless books and articles on it and made it their life's work to analyze and examine the subject. How would I reduce it to a twenty-minute mind-blowing speech at a cocktail event that connected the speaker's experience to a smart and original point of view and kept the schmoozers engaged? The last thing we wanted was to make her sound like an academic. I reserve that for the porn stars.

Feminism, race, power—it's not often I'm thrown an immense and unwieldy theme and given free rein to find and define the point of view or call to action, but despite the frustration and stress I know it brings, I savor the opportunity to tangle with such a vast-ranging subject. In cases such as these, The Point of the speech can emerge at any moment in the process. With Mimi, I found it on the Crazy Wall.

In the exploration stage, I had galloped along the endless mesa of the internet and learned all about the Alamo, where the event would be held. But I hadn't given much thought to Texas itself. I stared at the word "Texas," then scanned the wall, and noticed her decades-long work in the community— and it suddenly dawned on me that there was a connection! Texas is the Lone Star State and home to a few important feminist trailblazers, but what was a single star without its constellation? If the lone stars of Texan feminist history were iconic figures like Ann Richards, Liz Smith, and Molly Ivins, what did that mean for the rest of the women in the room and women across the country? Mimi might not be written about in the history books, but did that make her contribution any less valid? The concept of the "lone star" became the setup for a very active speech that gave all the women in the room a stake in the future of women's equity.

It's not hard to see what makes Texans so unique and independent in spirit. But thinking about my trip back to the

Lone Star State for this event, it got me thinking about the tough-talking, sharpshooting lone stars of the feminist movement. Women who, like Ann Richards, have in some way helped shape the discourse on sexism and the fight for equality in America. They are icons. They are warriors. They fight through activism, through art, through politics, and through leadership to break down the barriers that have held women back for centuries from fulfilling their potential and contributing to society. They are the women who change laws and who flip the bird at anyone who says "you can't." The Gloria Steinems and RBGs, the Sheryl Sandbergs and Beyoncés, the Serena Williamses and Sally Rides. We all have our own personal favorites. Who inspires you? I'd love to hear a few names.

All these women are trailblazers. They remind us what we can aspire to; they pave the way and inspire us to follow.

But there is another type of heroine. One who is maybe less visible than, say, Harriet Tubman or Hillary Clinton but every bit as important. She doesn't have to inspire millions of women to make a difference. She doesn't have to be a warrior or a leader. She doesn't have to wear feminist T-shirts if she doesn't want to. She doesn't have to want to be CEO or president of the United States. She doesn't have to organize a march on Washington. Hell, she doesn't even have to go if she can't make it work with her schedule—though it's cooler if she can. She is not a superstar, and her achievements are not necessarily quantifiable by a book deal or a Wikipedia page. No one may ever write about her. Or build statues in her memory—which is a shame, because boy, do we need some more female statues in this country. Her work is brave but it doesn't make headlines. It's high stakes but there is no single moment of victory. Until she is asked to speak at a company like this one!

She is you. And she is me.

I'm here tonight to remind you that championing gender equality isn't reserved for the lone star heroines. Because at its core, feminism is about being inspired by each other and being inspiring for each other.

The speech went on to outline the ways in which all women, regardless of power, seniority, or visibility, can actively change and shape the future. And at the end, the conclusion was set up with a fascinating tidbit I'd discovered while researching and rabbit-holing:

In the seventeenth century a Dutch scientist made a fascinating discovery: the king bee had ovaries! As is all too often the case, scientists had assumed that since it was the most important bee, it must be a man. But to their credit, the correction was made almost immediately. The king bee became the queen.

Wouldn't it be great if the same were true for us? "Oops, we were wrong—you guys have totally been in charge all along."

Unfortunately, we'll have to wait a while for that one.

In the meantime, though, we have so much to do. Be inspired, act, and show other women like you that you see what they're doing too and you applaud them. You don't have to be a lone star; you can be part of the dazzling constellation that illuminates the endless horizon.

I say let's amplify that idea by raising our glasses

and toasting to the future. It's bright. And there are way fewer people looking at nudie pictures at the desk next to yours.

When you know the precise angle and argument of your speech, the Crazy Wall is also where you find the outline, or what I prefer to call the beats. Not the beats in your headphones, the beats of the narrative. Writing a speech without the beats, the outline, is one of the biggest mistakes you can make. The beats are the stepping-stones that get you from the opening to the close. Imagine a river too wide and wild to swim. Take the East River, for example—too wide, too polluted, too swift a current, and too full of dead bodies. Imagine there are no bridges crossing this East River. No jet skis or sailing boats rented by young prepsters drunk on frozé. No police boats to help, no ferries. In crossing this disgusting yet majestic river without stepping-stones, you'd be washed away by the current in minutes and who knows where you might end up—maybe Connecticut, maybe New Jersey. Neither is ideal if you want to be in New York City.

Figuring out the beats of your speech, just as you would in writing a piece of fiction, is an essential part of the process, but whereas in fiction you invent the beats of the story, in speechwriting the invention is in how each beat pushes you to the next and to the next. This is the part of the journey where the real creativity is.

When we think of novelists, we liken them to artists. We see them as people with an enviable imagination and creative expression. Not so for a speechwriter. But this is an oversight, in my opinion. (Of course, I am an artiste!) Putting the speech together at this stage, working out what happens when and how it leads on to what, requires the same imagination and courage in challenging the audience.

So your unorthodox, crowd-thrilling pièce de résistance must start somewhere. But if there's no prescriptive or recommended outline technique, how do you know which Post-it on your Crazy Wall goes first? Certainly the worst thing you can do in my book is begin by saying, "Hi, my name is so-and-so and I'm the whatever of that organization you don't know" or "Hi, my name is so-and-so, I'm so-and-so's best friend, I've known her since we were in high school." Argh, so boring! And also, no one cares—get on with the speech!

You might have read somewhere that the best way to start a speech is to ask the crowd a question so that they're pulled into the experience from the top. I'm of the opinion that more effective than asking a question is asking yourself what, given everything you know about the type of speech you're about to write, you want the audience to *feel* right away and which story or data point or truth best illustrates the central point of your argument while delivering this effect. If you still want to use a question to deliver this, then at least you've done the thinking and it's intentional.

I often kick off a speech with an icebreaker, and though I'm always reluctant to advise memorization, a seemingly off-the-cuff joke at the outset that sounds spontaneous and is tied to the very thing the audience experienced before you started speaking—five other talking heads, a musical interlude, a stint at the bar—is always a winning play. It's kind of like a false start. You can still begin with something powerful, even serious, once you've taken a breath after the joke, but it helps reassure the crowd that they're not going to feel desperately awkward for any extended length of time.

There is a hilarious episode of the radio show and podcast *This American Life* about fiascos in which the narrator puts the role of the audience as willing participants to the test in recalling a college theater production of *Peter Pan* he went to see when he was a student. In spite of being staged by a visiting and very ambitious artistic director, and even though there'd been weeks of rigorous rehearsal, on opening night, the show unravels scene by scene, one accident after another. Wendy, suspended from the ceiling by a very visible bungee cord, flies face-first into a set closet. Captain Hook's hook is flung into the audience thanks to the actor's wild gesticulations and on its descent punches an old lady in the gut. The disasters just keep mounting up. I remember so well listening to the story because I was running at the time and I was laughing so hard I had to stop just to avoid tripping over my feet. What is it about laughter that renders the body so limp? Forty minutes of destruction and chaos later, the narrator describes the inflection point where the audience, a previously benign force who have been courteous and kind for the most part, trying hard to exercise restraint and decorum and lean on their empathy for these poor performers, can do so no longer. Their loyalty has reached its breaking point. And from one moment to the next their most animalistic instincts are unleashed, transforming them from allies to savages panting for more drama. By the end of the play, with firefighters on the scene and on the stage, their cruel laughter is unbridled and unstoppable.

I always tell my clients that audiences want you to succeed; it's a much better experience for them if you do. But it is true that once you lose them, it's very hard to win them back, so it pays to earn some reserves of loyalty any way you can.

In Peggy Noonan's *On Speaking Well*, the author recalls an icebreaker a friend of hers wrote for her in anticipation of an upcoming appearance for a political group in New York. "I knew what I wanted to say about politics but I couldn't think of anything that would make the audience laugh," she writes.

So I called a friend of mine and said, "Help." He asked for the specifics of the event. It's a dinner, I said, at the Waldorf. About four hundred people, they're sophisticated, it's a fancy event. The mayor will be there, he speaks after me, I introduce him.

My friend went off to think. A few days later he called. "Did you see the picture of Giuliani at the press club thing the other night?" I had. Mayor Giuliani had taken part in a press club skit and had come out onto the stage in full drag—blond wig, big eyelashes, long beaded dress. The pictures were all over the papers, and they were particularly striking because Giuliani looked not so much amusing as real weird.

"This is the joke," said my friend. "You stand up there and say, 'It's wonderful to be in the Waldorf, in this lovely and elegant room. I was so excited by the prospect, and by seeing all of you, that I was going to get all decked out in a beautiful gown. But I didn't want to take the chance of showing up in the same thing the mayor might be wearing, so—"

I used it and it got a big laugh.

I remember reading this and raising an eyebrow, specifically the right one, because the left never seems to want to budge. I was surprised—not, of course, by the description of Rudy Giuliani in drag, since we all know how he likes his hair dye, but because, though I would never snub a trailblazer like Noonan, she hadn't thought to do this herself. I would bet that if she'd thought about it, she too would have been able to craft the joke. It simply didn't occur to her.

During the initial phase of due diligence, I always make it my business to find out how many people and who specifically might be speaking before my client, and if there is any other kind of prelude to their star moment. This is good practice, and not just for humor's sake. In a more corporate setting, if my client is being introduced or if there is literature made available detailing their professional accomplishments, it excuses us from the mind-melting resume download, and fast-tracks us to the ideas and stories and insights that are a consequence of this experience. It also means that in the middle of the narrative we don't have to stop to give background. Everyone already knows you founded an orphanage in Kenya, so you can get right to talking about the kid who just graduated from college.

If a particularly brilliant or well-known speaker is appearing before you, look them up. Use what you already know, fear, or admire about them, or what you desire or expect from them. This is where self-deprecation can work nicely for you; you don't need to be British. If what precedes you is a chorus line doing a number, think about your relationship to music, dance, and theater. If what comes on before you is a heart-wrenching video of orphaned children, acknowledge where the audience may be emotionally directly following that experience—perhaps not with a joke but with some humility and gratitude for their continued attention. No jokes about orphaned children, please. Whatever the tone of that initial remark, should you choose to use one, currying the favor of the audience early will take you far. And there I was thinking I'd moved on from curry.

For an ambitious speaker (which I have no doubt you are), there's an even more cunning move you can make when it comes to the opening bit, and that is exploring how you can bring it full circle at the end. This is sometimes referred to as the "bookend," and if you can employ the device effectively, it makes you sound very smart indeed, which is the whole point of speaking in public, isn't it? You see this device in all types of storytelling. To give you something familiar, let's return to *The Breakfast Club*, the movie that taught me about weed, tampons, PB&J, and Mr. Rogers—all things you should know at eleven years old.

For anyone who hasn't seen it even once, the film opens with a vignette of high schoolers arriving for detention on a Saturday morning. Through a brief exchange between each character and the parent doing the drop-off before the kid gets out of the car, the audience understands very quickly the high school stereotype into which the character fits—the jock, the prom queen, the weirdo, the nerd, the fuck-up. At the end of the movie we return to this conceit: parents, cars, students. Except now the parents are picking up kids who, after spending an entire day in a room together, have all undergone a profound transformation and whom the audience have gotten to know as well-intentioned and complex young people. The story has evolved, and we see this through the same narrative device. God, I'm tearing up just playing it in my mind. It's so good.

In a speech, you can do exactly the same, and I would say I do it about 85 percent of the time.

To use an example of someone you already know, let's take Ken's speech. We've already established that this comprised personal anecdotes with an abundance of industry insight. Now I can show you what that looked like as it opened and concluded.

> *When I was asked to speak today on the future of cool, I was flattered. Me, cool? I thought. Why, thank you, I'd love to! And then I took a selfie to mark the occasion.*
>
> *I'm such a millennial.*
>
> *I'm not sure that they meant the compliment quite the way I took it, but I'd like to think the reason I'm here today talking to such an esteemed group of industry experts is because I have a pretty cool story to tell. . . .*
>
> *I grew up on a remote farm in a small town where the elders of the farming community reminded me often enough that I didn't belong. It was okay—I knew early on, when the tacky decor in the living room started bothering me, that they were right. So when I was fifteen, I ran away from home. For the next couple of years I bounced between selling MCI long-distance phone service, shifts at Applebee's, the graveyard shift at the Git-N-Go gas station, and many different other dead-end jobs. And for a while I'd sleep in my car, which, by the way, is NOT a good alternative to a convertible bed no matter which way you arrange the pillows.*

The "Crazy Wall"

The turning point came in 1999 when one day a friend asked me to pick her up and give her a ride to work. That short journey from her house to her office was life-changing. The route I usually took was blocked, and when I tried an alternate route it was blocked too. I tried a third street, and—blocked. I sat in my car and looked around at my options and I saw clearly that I didn't have any. That notion crystallized so clearly in my mind in that instant. I had no options where I was and I needed to get out of there fast. That night I sold my DVD collection and used it to rent a moving truck, and within twenty-four hours of deciding I had to leave, I was on the road and on my way to starting the life I now have today.

Ken seamlessly segued into a quick recap of his professional ascent and what he had learned. The speech centered on three big takeaways he imparted to his audience, and for each he broke it out and elaborated on its import for the future of homebuilding for the next generation. This is how he ended:

Millennials—my peers—they need options. We don't want them sitting in their Ubers looking out the window and seeing only dead ends, like I did. Because if they don't move; if they continue renting because they're not being offered what they want from a purchase, the homebuilding industry will be bulldozed to the ground. It sounds dramatic. But hey, I ran away and lived in a car. I'm into drama.

And I know the value of a home.

I'm not saying this speech had anything to do with what happened to his career next, but I will say that people kept listening to what he had to say and now he's a TV star.

The Crazy Wall isn't so crazy when you account for its value to your process. Throwing things up, making a mess, and then starting to make sense of it all can be one of the most gratifying moments—if you've really earned it. If you've worked hard enough to unearth the best material and you've opened your mind to the possibilities of where it can take you by reflecting on the content with a fresh perspective, it's highly likely that your outline and its beats will start looking very different from what you'd thought it might at the outset, regardless of whether you started at Burna Boy or Yo-Yo Ma.

7

The Reinvented Wheel

Navigating the Vexing (and Vital)
Pursuit of Originality

At the eleventh hour, as Nathan's surprise fortieth-birthday party approached, I realized I still hadn't written his speech. It had been on my list of to-dos behind finalizing the open bar, haggling over the cost of pigs in a blanket, and orchestrating the big moment when Nathan arrived at what he thought would be a Christmas dinner with four Brit friends at a gastropub only to be ushered into a private room where sixty friends shouted, "Sham sham woowee woowee." (I'll explain that part later, I promise.)

I had intended to mount an elaborate showcase with Nathan's theater friends. The aim was to craft a speech that was punctuated by funny sets and sketches, and I'd reached out to a specific group a month earlier to begin brainstorming. Then the pigs in their blankets got in the way and my ambitious plan was thwarted. On the day before the December 22 party I sat with my head bursting full of things I knew I wanted to say about my beloved husband but knowing too that because I'm a speechwriter, the pressure was on to deliver something excellent, or at least something effortless.

I'll tell you a secret that won't help most people: if you're a capable performer, you can easily disguise a mediocre speech, which is exactly why I believe Meghan Markle's UN speech in 2015 was such a hit. It began with a beautiful story about how as a young girl she was enraged by a dishwashing liquid commercial that had pigeonholed women as housewives whose lives revolved around cleaning the kitchen. With the encouragement of her now estranged father she wrote letters to the most important person she could think of (at the time this person was Hillary Clinton) and to the CEO of the company that made the soap. Lo and behold, weeks later the tagline for the product's commercial was suddenly changed to include men as well. It was, I confess, a fabulous story bubbling over with aspiration and innocence. But you'd be forgiven for not having noticed the soup of clichés that followed, disguised as it was by the exceptional presentation Markle was able to give her audience. She's an actress, so it comes with the territory, but not all actors are great speakers. We've all seen the Oscar duds—I'm sure I don't need to convince you. Markle, however, performed in such a way that even the most cynical spectator (me) dying to decry her inauthenticity could barely find fault.

Now, I may not match your estimation of Meghan Markle, or maybe you loathe the British monarchy and I exceed it, but I did go to drama school and live the happiest days of my life at that point reciting Shakespeare and Mamet and prancing to musical numbers from *West Side Story*, so I wasn't too worried about the delivery of Nathan's speech. In this endeavor, though, I was determined that the script itself be the showstopper rather than the performance. I wanted to find a way to fit all of Nathan's unique qualities into the unique narrative he deserved—something more interesting than "what a great guy." With originality in my mind's eye I began to search the disparate and random facts about him, looking for a novel angle I might take.

It occurred to me that while I had so much to say about Nathan, I had only known him for a quarter of his life so far, and that many people who'd be at the party—family, college friends, and so on—knew him in ways I never would. As I held this idea in my mind, something scribbled on a sticky note on my Crazy Wall caught my eye. It was in a subcategory of Truths I'd labeled Things That Drive Me Nuts About Nathan. In this subcategory there was only one note. So far. Remember the secret storage unit with the embarrassing costumes that I mentioned in Chapter 1? I didn't make that up—it's Nathan's. Since I've known him he has paid an exorbitant rent to Manhattan Mini Storage, and every month I nag him about what the hell is in this mysterious unit and when he's going to empty it. At the time of writing this is still the case, and I imagine not much will change in the coming years. What a brilliant analogy, I thought, for someone whose life is not entirely known to me. And when I considered that the storage unit would provide a fun and unexpected opener that I knew would suit the celebratory ambience, it all began to fit together. I should mention that the aim was to roast him to cinders. In my opinion, if you're not going to make people laugh, you have no right to interrupt a party.

Somewhere in the city there is a Manhattan Mini Storage space paid for every month by one Nathan Phillips.

*This Nathan would be quick to set you straight—he's
not to be confused with the swarthy Australian actor best
known from a memorable performance in* Snakes on
a Plane. *Rather, he is a more hirsute gent from New
England—a sensitive and soft-spoken chap known less
for his surf skills and six-pack than for his unique ability to mime pretty much everything he says with his
hands while he's saying it, and his incredibly short legs
when compared to his torso.*

*This Nathan Phillips may not be able to save you
from poisonous reptiles thirty thousand feet in the sky,
but he can save an awkward moment with a comic one-
liner and make the moment that much more awkward.
Yes, ladies and gentlemen, I'm talking about the Nathan
Phillips you all know and love—the friend who will always "freshen your cocktail" even when you're drinking
a beer, the brother who will forget your birthday every
year but loves you just as much as the last, the father
who plays satanic metal to his three-year-old when his
wife isn't around, and the husband who always warns
me when he's forgotten to take his Lactaid. It is this
Nathan Phillips who owns the storage unit somewhere
in Manhattan.*

The next beat came naturally. Why hadn't he emptied
the storage unit yet? That was an obvious next question,
and the answer gave me another chance to continue the
deluge. Notice the tone is heightened, as if in the style of
an English folk tale—this was less of a choice than a natural progression from the first line about a "chap named
Nathan Phillips."

Now, in the eight years that Nathan and I have been to-gether, he hasn't visited this storage unit once. He could have transferred the contents to the loft in our apart-ment. Or he could have brought home a selection of high school swimming trophies to sandwich between his Barry Manilow records and the stack of stereos from the seventies that don't work but effectively disguise our mass-produced bourgeois West Elm shelving. And yet . . . he has done neither.

Why? I can assure you his neglect bears no relation to the value of the contents. Indeed this unit is stuffed full of photographs and artifacts collected over the forty years that Nathan has spent dancing, prancing, miming, and dare I say bullshitting his way through the world. From Fall River to Emerson to San Francisco to New York, the stories are all in there. It's a treasure trove of fond mem-ories and oddities.

No, the reason he hasn't been to empty out its contents is my fault.

You see, I love Nathan very much. But I don't know if my love needs to be tested by pictures of him with wavy waist-length hair sporting loads of earrings and a sec-ondhand pair of clogs; or by reminders of any of his old wardrobe, so much of which was brown and made of flammable material. Or by improv props like the lifelike set of rubber boobs that somehow managed to fall out of his cupboard while prospective tenants looked around our old apartment. Me mumbling, "Oh, sometimes he dresses up as women" did little to temper their shock.

I also don't necessarily need to see how many other random headshots he's collected of actors whose names

*he thinks are funny. For eight precious years we've been
arguing about whether he can get the picture of one of his
favorites tattooed on his arm, and I've finally won. This
total stranger's name is already Nathan's password to
every important account he holds—his Regal Crown
Club movie account, Amazon Prime, Nespresso, and,
of course, Planned Parenthood.*

This admission of guilt and denial then led me to a plain
truth: that I didn't need these tangible mementos to tell me
who Nathan used to be, because along with the artifacts collected over years, Nathan had also kept every single one of
his friends, and they had already provided me with ample
recollection of Nathan's not-quite-sordid past. This was the
section where I was able to hand the narrative reins over to
his friends. I hadn't managed to pull off the sketch idea but
I had asked them each to send one line or paragraph about
Nathan—something that summarized their experience of
him—that I could read out loud. The stories and quotes were
hilarious; everyone had put their best foot forward, knowing
the favor I had asked was small and low stakes for them.

Transitioning from these reviews was then easy. And this
is where the speech changed gear just a touch. While I never
let go of the humor and energy, I wanted to make sure Nathan knew how awed I was by him.

*There are just so many tales because Nathan has done
more in his forty years than Kirk Douglas has in a
hundred. Kirk has made eighty-five movies, I heard on
the radio yesterday. But count Nathan's masterpieces:*
Massholia, Field of Mars, My Lie Story, The Fastest

Man in the World (Generally Speaking), How to Date Women, The Internet Comedy Show, Sex You I'm Gonna, Lactose Intolerant: A Short Play, *all the mime stuff . . . And then there are the characters he has played: Jerry di Brugugliuglio, Percy Bollocks, Aristotle Narcisssus. Not to mention the awesome work in technology and advertising that has actually been noticed by people outside of his immediate circle of friends and The PIT:*

Inside the Blue, The And, *and his most recent pièce de résistance, R—a film about virtual reality, which, I don't mind telling you, has been selected to play at Sundance.*

There is simply no one, at least no one I know, who has the imagination, the intelligence, the endless curiosity, the sense of humor, the patience, the ability to just keep making stuff, and the stamina he does—except when it comes to driving on the highway, when he mysteriously develops narcolepsy and insists I take the wheel.

Being married to Nathan is really hard work. Because every day he challenges me to be better than I was the day before, to be less reluctant, more open-minded, to do the things I want to do but am too scared to, and to trust that other people can help me get there.

Baby, there isn't a storage space in this city big enough for the memories I hope to make with you as we get old together. Well, as I get old—you're already there.

So here's to you, Nathan Phillips, a most swarthy forty-year-old who, despite a receding hairline, proves it's never too late to start eating chicken again. Cheers!

I always tell clients who are speaking about people they love that if the whole speech is slushy, it begins to sound gratuitous. When I turned directly to Nathan right at the end and showed vulnerability in my adoration for him, the moment felt very real, I think, for the people in the room. And I made good on The Oratory Laboratory full-circle rule by bringing it back to the Nathan Phillips theme while squeezing in one more joke that everyone in the room would understand: his recent and well-documented return to carnivorism after twenty years as a vegetarian.

Originality must be a north star for any speechwriter, and, I would hope, for any speaker. After all, if you're not original, why would anyone be compelled to listen to what you have to say? But new perspectives and new ideas are practically impossible to come by, so focusing on that can be intimidating. The guy who did his TED talk about how creativity is as important as education for children was not the first person to think this. The woman talking about bamboo as a building material did not discover bamboo. What matters is the way you convey your perspective with personal, specific, and original language. To me, that's what the craft of speechwriting is all about. It's the how, not the what.

At the heart of The Oratory Laboratory process is a promise that we never recycle material. I'm a keen recycler in domestic life—you can't unsee the garbage island. But fodder for speeches is the only material I will never reuse, especially between speakers. This isn't just because I want to make sure every speech is bespoke and authentic to the speaker. It's because I want to be original and do something that hasn't been done before. It's a challenge I take seriously and one that clients find hard to stomach sometimes. It's probably tied up in my own need to push buttons and break boundaries—to be able to say, "There, I told you I could do it." But I don't see that as a selfish quality if someone else reaps the rewards. Being bold and putting yourself out there, versus just doing the "acceptable thing" and getting it over with, takes confidence and courage. In my opinion there is no such thing as "acceptable" or "correct" and no one becomes "unforgettable" for simply meeting expectations.

There are many ways in which to innovate and create something that authentically captures the imagination of the people on the receiving end. Playing and experimenting at the Crazy Wall certainly opens you up to original ideas in terms of the narrative arc, and it can be instrumental in defining a specific angle that hopefully hasn't been heard before. But when we think of originality, it helps to return again to the audience and ask how you can make their experience of your speech unlike anything else they may have encountered. To do this requires more than imagination and ingenuity. In order to unleash our potential, we should embrace our natural inclination to be daring, not smother it.

You might hear all this and consider it bluster. Maybe you'll ask, "Well, what was so daring about Martin Luther King Jr.'s 'I Have a Dream' speech?" To which I'd say, beyond the depiction of racial harmony it dared to imagine, you only have to watch video of the March on Washington 2020 and notice that while the speakers all had the best intentions, no one delivered a dream, as King did in 1963. King wrote his speech in a moment when much of the nation was crying out for a moral reckoning. He pitted oppression against freedom, love against hate. He didn't write a speech; he leaned on his work in the church and wrote a sermon for America.

In March 2018, at another momentous rally, hundreds of thousands of people from across the country gathered in Washington, DC, to join the teenage organizers of March for Their Lives. At the end of the event, Emma Gonzalez took the stage and spoke about the horrors of the mass shooting that had taken place at Marjory Stoneman Douglas High School. For two minutes she spoke about her friends, and then for four minutes—the length of time the gunman had spent massacring them one by one—she was silent. Standing on the podium in front of all those people, she looked fierce and yet so very vulnerable. Four minutes is excruciatingly long to be mute. And yet the silence was, to resort to cliché, deafening. Extraordinarily so.

I consider these kinds of courageous diversions from the norm as innovating within the format of the speech itself. Beyond a bewitching storyline and a clever narrative structure, the speaker changes the very shape of the speech and in doing so alters its chemistry. When I think of format, I'm thinking of something clearly recognizable as "different" when reviewed alongside a more traditional speech with a beginning, middle, and end. I'm thinking of how we can employ unexpected elements and tools to make something new, just like an artist might cover their canvas with such thick paint that the resulting work appears sculptural, not merely two-dimensional.

The next thing I'm going to say is about Phil Collins, which I'm pretty sure you're not expecting. Surprise! Originality! If you've never heard "In the Air Tonight," go now and pull it up on whatever streaming service you use. If you're at home and have vinyl, even better. You should know I wrote the rest of this chapter with that song on repeat. Why? Well, no one needs a reason to listen to Phil Collins, but in this case it's because the song embodies the concept of structural novelty.

For almost its entirety the song lingers in an electronic mist, Collins crooning over the top, until, approaching the fourth minute, when you think you understand the journey you're on and expecting its impending eighties fade-out, boom! A huge percussive beat rips through the keyboards and Collins's echo-enhanced vocals. Minute four! That's not how songs are meant to go. It literally begins as the song is about to end. But this off-the-wall structure is what makes it a legendary track.

If you're more of a cinephile, you might remember the first time you saw the movie *Memento*. It was a story told backward, and we'd never seen anything like it. The most boundary-pushing makers—from Marina Abramovic with her interactive pieces to J. J. Abrams and his co-authored novel *S*, which includes supplementary materials and clues—dare to mess not just with the contents but with the very thing that contains them. With "In the Air Tonight," Collins is still putting out a tune. *Memento* is still a movie. But both challenge the conventions of their storytelling media.

Some of my favorite speeches have been those where a bold client has allowed me to play around with format. Take, for example, a speech I wrote for Brooke, a self-described "boss lady" and bona fide influencer. We'd worked together before and I knew her well from other areas of my life, so when she was asked to speak at an Ivy League school about the convergence of technology and advertising, I knew she'd be game to try something different. I read and reread her ad agency's capabilities decks and her own writing about a personal strategy she believed kept her at the forefront of her industry. There were a few routes we could have taken, but we decided a speech about "white space" would be appropriate for this young crowd of creative ingenues. White space, as Brooke describes it, is the unlikely, unexplored space where opportunity beckons. It's not, as we quipped at the time, the front-row seating at a Trump rally. Knowing that the gist of the speech was that white space is a space for unlikely connections—not dissimilar from the Crazy Wall in spirit—I had an idea about how to get the audience playing with white space too. And knowing that Brooke wasn't afraid of breaking with convention I knew she'd be on board. The beginning of her speech explained the premise:

> *The white space I'm talking about has no convention—no rules, no precedent. It is territory unexplored. It is the opportunity to tell new stories in ways previously unimagined. It is where, as storytellers, we innovate.*
>
> *It's this. [She holds up a blank piece of paper.]*
> *The blank page where my story hasn't yet been told. I can do anything here. It's open season. I could put words on it and read you my ideas, right? That's what most people do in these situations. That's what your professors are hoping I've done, I'm sure. And, well, considering the amount of content I have to share, it's not a bad idea. So here it is: my speech. [She holds up another page.] Written down thought for thought, just like it should be. My colleague is handing out copies of the whole text for you to follow. You could totally just take it away*

now if you want and read it in your own time. And if you choose to do so, I'll wish you all the best—the font is pretty damn small. But I'd love for you to stay and follow along with me. Because I want to do something different with this story. I want to find a way to make you a part of my story. To use the white space to create something unique, that only we could do together. I want you to follow my speech, but it's up to you to decide how you want to do that. All I ask is that you try to keep up.

As the talk progressed Brooke invited the audience to follow instructions projected behind her at specific moments in the speech, to fold and manipulate the paper step by step. By the end they had created a beautiful origami dragon out of the paper. It was a metaphorical rendering of white space, and it was a hit.

I can't always push originality on speakers, especially those who are regulars on the keynote circuit. I accept that a particular storyline might well be appealing to more than one audience, and for the sake of sanity, you cannot reinvent the wheel every time you're a guest speaker at a business luncheon. I'm also keenly aware that there are industry leaders out there who peddle the same message with the same takeaways because they are specifically asked to do so. But at some point even that story has to change.

I was approached at one time by one such pioneer, Sara Blakely of Spanx, whose internal communications team admitted she'd used the same story and the same building blocks for over ten years and needed a refresh. I would have enjoyed working with her—who doesn't love a control top and a heroine? It was an opportune moment for the company to undertake a revamp, since Kim Kardashian had just launched her own line of figure-hugging underwear (perhaps it was even the motivation), but, sadly, I never got my hands on that underwear. I'll never know why. Perhaps she wasn't quite as drawn to the dollar figure I was proposing. Or perhaps my spiel about doing something truly different just seemed a little too fringe when compared to other powerhouse communications agencies whose proposals likely offered something neater and more comfortable. A more Spanx-esque approach, you might say.

Daring is in the eye of the beholder, of course, and while I don't always get to execute my wildest vision for a speech, I've managed to persuade a satisfying number of speakers to strive for originality over safety. For example, for a father of the bride who loved to listen to the Beatles with his daughter, I reimagined a Beatles compilation album that correlated to her personality traits and his favorite stories about her; he made the playlist, and the speech was an explanation of the song list.

For the "best woman" of a groom who worked in consumer packaging, we created a unique barcode after I'd noticed on the Crazy Wall that there were a lot of specific dates and enumerable items in the anecdotes and facts she'd provided. At the start of the speech she revealed a large banner with this barcode, black lines and all. At this point she started to explain the numbers:

> *Nineteen-ninety-eight was the year I met Michael for the first time in a house share in Martha's Vineyard. We had a friend in common and spent a good portion of the summer hanging out. I remember thinking that he*

*was super high energy, very charming but definitely a
bit too keen on his bicycle.*

*Seven was the number of times a week that Michael
would try to convince all of us to go on an all-day bike
ride. [She pointed to a 0] This was the number of times
we said yes.*

For a groom who insisted on speaking not once, not twice,
but three times during his wedding weekend in the Berkshires,
I suggested we craft for his first speech a phony analysis of
his DNA that he read out for his new wife, a genetics re-
searcher. The conceit was that he'd sent off a blood sample
so that she had one final opportunity to bail on the wedding
if she knew exactly what she had coming down the pipeline
in terms of male pattern baldness, arthritis, and so on. Since
he was twenty years her senior, it worked really well. I would
never normally suggest a groom make himself the subject
of a speech, but I worked very hard to ensure that he was
self-deprecating to a fault (there was plenty of material to
use, believe me), that wherever possible he used his point to
bring it back to the bride, and, most importantly, that it was
funny throughout. It had to make everyone laugh all the
time. There could be no other reason to speak a third time
other than to make merry.

Thinking outside the box is not a novel concept, and yet
with speeches it seems confined to poorly executed renditions
of well-known songs, awkwardly rapped A-to-Z's, or the "I've
got it—let's use a slide show of embarrassing photos!" idea.
The year *Hamilton* debuted on Broadway, for instance, I had
my hands full gently telling overexcited maids of honor that
doing their speech to Angelica Schuyler's maid-of-honor

toast number was clichéd and humiliating. I had the conversation so many times I only had to roll my eyes on a phone call and my account manager would understand that we had another one on the line.

Two young finance guys who we'll call Sy and Ali didn't want *Hamilton,* but they did want rap and they ignored my repeated attempts of discouragement. Two-handers demand ingenuity by definition. When we get requests for multiple speakers I will always warn them that the very first priority is to make sure that whatever we do, it is not going to be a speech with the parts divvied up and distributed to each speaker willy-nilly. The roles of each player are considered. And the conceit is specific to the subject of the speech. I've had three teenage kids "find" their mother's diary and use that to craft a narrative around all the things she does for them (and for herself). Most important is that these kinds of speeches feel like dialogues and dynamic exchanges between speakers—they feed off each other, speak over each other if that's their tendency. It's never just a question of "you take this line and I'll take that one."

Sy and Ali, however, weren't just making a joint speech. Eager to make connections with Wall Street's biggest movers and shakers, they had been nominated to join a clandestine fraternity and were facing their hazing at the secret circle's annual event at the St. Regis Hotel. They needed a showstopper if they wanted to avoid being pelted with tomatoes and booed offstage. A *New York Times* reporter had crashed this audacious and indulgent event a few years prior and exposed the group as an upper-crust social club where the latest financial and political scandals were fodder for bawdy show tunes and parodies of liberal issues. I could attest to that—this was the second time I'd had to put my liberal agenda aside and make jokes about the 99 percent for the participants.

Sy, Ali, and I talked a lot about the themes that would go into the piece: Hillary's emails, Wilbur Ross's disappearing millions, the Panama Papers, Roy Moore, even Hurricane Maria (yes, really). I suggested we re-create Johnny Cash's "Folsom Prison Blues." Ali would be jailed as part of the Muslim ban and Sy for insider trading. The song would be instantly familiar to the audience, and the time signature of the song was easy for two people who, I had surmised, had no sense of rhythm. But they wanted something "cooler." And so they insisted on doing a version of Jay-Z's "Empire State of Mind." I said no. I said pleeeease no. But they wanted it.

I will readily confess that while I suspected they were setting themselves up for a tomato pelting, I had a fantastic time rewriting the lyrics of the iconic tune. When I was a teenager, I listened to a lot of hip-hop and R&B on my stacked CD player, and as a writer today, the marriage of a skilled lyricist and a good beat both inspires and provokes envy in equal measure. I heard a segment on the radio the other day with a George Washington University professor who believes Jay-Z to be the modern-day Robert Frost. Well, I may be able to perform like Ms. Markle, but I'm no poet like Jay-Z, and I can tell you it was hard to get the timing right with the new lyrics, harder still to get Sy and Ali in sync. The night of their delivery session, we sat around an enormous conference table at one of the biggest private equity firms in the city, fifty floors above Fifth Avenue, and as I marveled at the twinkling lights of midtown's high-rise offices I tried to concentrate on the task at hand. Sy and Ali were on their feet giving it their best, using slides and a karaoke-style app to guide them through the customized script. My skills were a closer match to Jay Z's at least, than theirs.

Of course it was all in good fun, but deep down, every guy wants to be able to rap like "Hov," and it's hard to disguise that. In the end, they fell into the same trap so many others do: they'd picked a song they liked rather than a song that made sense for the moment. There's being clever and there's being gimmicky, and there's a fine line between the two. If you find yourself using a stunt or shtick that has nothing to tie it specifically to you or the subject of your speech, you can be sure you're veering into the gimmicky. And with that I'll tell you that "Sham sham woowee woowee," while a ridiculous way to greet a forty-year-old man, is a well-known Nathan Phillips song lyric that made it into many an original number back in his performing days. Very silly, but very specific.

8

The Thing That Happened

How Your Stories Serve Your Speech

'll never forget the time my friend Cami and I planned a two-month trip around Southeast Asia. We had methodically and painstakingly plotted every stop, every beach, every hostel, and every splurge on a decent hotel for a hot shower and a night of cable TV. By the time departure day arrived, I'd had my backpack packed for over a week. All I had to do in the morning was check for the twentieth time that my contact lenses and passport were in there—the two things you can't really buy from a street seller in Thailand unless you want to go nowhere fast with conjunctivitis.

Cami and I met on the subway and got to the airport with plenty of time to spare. She'd drawn up an airport itinerary to allow us enough time to check in and then spend a while browsing through the magazines at Hudson News—Cami loves all things beauty and "insider" as long as what's inside are free samples tucked between the pages of glossy photoshoots. She even made time for a revolting airport breakfast where we would toast our departure with a coffee that would taste like a New York City puddle and freedom all at once.

But as we were ushered toward the airline's check-in desk, I noticed Cami's face turning a weird shade of puce. I thought she might be about to throw up. She had, after all, spent the night before with her new boyfriend, whom I definitely found sickening. Don't worry, I'm not talking about the groom. But as she rummaged through her carry-on bag I knew that it wasn't the corny boyfriend that was the cause of the nausea. She'd forgotten her passport.

Reacting with the electric charge of a hired assassin in a Netflix thriller, she pushed me up to the check-in desk, yelled, "Grab me a *Marie Claire*!," and disappeared into an Uber, whose previous passenger was still trying to wrest his bags from the trunk. She made it to her apartment and back in time to grab an airport muffin from the Euro Cafe that tasted like socks, and then off we headed to Singapore with twenty-plus hours to recover from the trauma. Thank God for those sample-sized facial treatments in Cami's magazines.

That's actually not my story. It is a highly embellished version of a client's account of a trip she took with her best friend, at whose wedding she was due to speak as maid of honor. I'd asked Emily to tell me a memorable story about her friend Cami, and the account she wrote down for me went something like this: "One time we went traveling together and when we got to the airport Cami realized she'd left her passport at home so she had to race back to get it. I was so nervous she was going to miss the flight, but she made it and we went on an amazing trip together. Phew!"

The memory had clearly resurfaced the sense of urgency and the hilarity of the situation for Emily, but when I read this, my own heart skipped not a beat. I could have taken a polygraph test, I was that calm. Though she believed the debacle to be a story worth regurgitating, I knew its use would be different from what she had in mind. To me it was a classic "you had to be there" moment—a significant memory of her relationship with Cami, but neither funny nor compelling enough for anyone else.

Our lives are for the most part made up of moments like this, moments that I like to call Things That Happen. Some are big, some are small, some are worth sharing, and others perhaps aren't. To connect with your audience in the most effective way, you must be able to distinguish between them, considering their limitations and possibilities.

You'll recall I warned you earlier, when talking about the categories on the Crazy Wall, about the subtleties of anecdotal material. Things That Happen is what I call the anecdotal material that fuels the connection and resonance with the audience. You might instinctively consider Things That Happen "stories."

Nowadays, stories serve as a tonic to many of humankind's woes and as a strategy for personal advancement. Can't get a promotion? Learn how to tell your story. Feeling directionless? Go on a storytelling retreat—revelations and hugging guaranteed. You can't go anywhere today—LinkedIn, the dog park, a cocktail party—without bumping into a self-proclaimed storyteller. But as the term gets thrown about and we're asked to apply the same expectations to a five-second Instagram "story" with sparkly emojis and hashtags as we are to a twelve-hour Ken Burns documentary, the universal definition is likely to splinter.

What is a story? And why does it matter that we draw any distinctions?

A story is a construct of our own design. It typically has a neat beginning, middle, and end. It is crafted with precision and consideration and is made up entirely of moments, or Things That Happen. It often comprises certain elements such as character and setting, but most importantly it must have high stakes and a resolution in which the protagonist undergoes some kind of transformation. If you happen to be, let's say, a filmmaker or a novelist, you know that creating a good story for a movie or book requires a tremendous amount of skill. If you are working with a shorter format, it doesn't mean that the thought process involved is less exacting. If you've ever tried to write a Moth story, you'll know how hard it is to create the tension in the right place and give the audience the right payoff while remaining honest about what actually happened.

When you're considering your anecdotal material for a speech and you think you might have a good story to tell, be warned: a naturally occurring story is rarely perfect. Even if you can point to a beginning, middle, and end, does the story promise the tension and the resolution your audience craves? Is it exciting? Funny? Urgent? And it's always worth asking yourself whether you've heard a similar story before, because if you have, that alone should cast suspicion on it.

As a stand-alone story, Emily's airport crisis was not enough of a debacle to warrant a full retelling. It didn't have any major stakes or a big transformative moment. Cami didn't miss the flight; she didn't have to go to Thailand by herself without a suitcase; she didn't meet her husband UberPooling on the way back home to pick up her passport. She just got on the plane as planned, albeit a little later. It was a pretty mundane tale that a lot of people could tell. I've definitely forgotten my passport and missed a flight. And it wasn't funny either. I had to turn Cami into a cartoon hero and dress up the account with invented Uber drivers and muffins to create drama.

But that didn't mean it wasn't very useful. As a Thing That Happened, we could still craft it into a rich and rewarding moment in the speech. If, for example, we wanted to describe Cami as unpredictable but resourceful, Emily could say: "I'm never sure how an adventure with Cami might turn out, or indeed if it will turn out at all, as I discovered the time she left her passport at home on the way to Thailand." Then we could use it again later as a bookend (remember those?): "One thing that isn't hard to predict is that a life with Cami will be a tremendous adventure." An alternative would be to kick off the speech with "My journey with Cami began in 1998 when we took a trip to Thailand and she forgot her passport," and then end it with a pre-honeymoon warning to the groom: "Your journey is just beginning. Brace yourself . . . and make sure she packs her passport."

As it turned out, in reality Cami was notoriously forgetful, so I repurposed the story as a punchline: ". . . as I discovered the day she forgot her passport on our trip to Thailand and had to drive at top speed back to Brooklyn to get it." And I linked it to the fact that Cami loved the New York subways: "That was one day she didn't wait for the A, C, or E." By itself the story wasn't much, but we used it wisely and got a good laugh.

A good speechwriter is, by definition, a good storyteller because a speech, in its totality, must also provide tension and an emotional release. It must be constructed thoughtfully, with a clever beginning and end. But contrary to what most people might think, you don't need a great story to make a great speech. A speech recognizes that the fragmented moments of people's lives—the Things That Happen—can be put to work just as effectively within a larger narrative. This kind of anecdotal material can explain a larger unrelated point—that is, it can serve as an analogy or a metaphor; it can introduce a theme or a new idea; prove an idea or point about something else; provide a framing device for the opening and closing of the speech; or provide a punchline for a joke. The smallest moments can be nuggets of narrative gold, and the big ones may well benefit from being dismantled and redistributed bit by bit throughout the speech. No matter how you use those moments, those stories, those Things That Happen, you must always be crystal clear on one thing: why they are in your speech.

Emily thought she had a story, but in fact, as we've established, what she had was a punchline. On the other hand, Dustin, a best man, recalled in an offhand manner a Thing That Happened that might at first have seemed quite ordinary. But when I instinctively nudged him for more information, it turned out to be so much more. Cracked open, it was a beautiful anecdote that provided a tight open and close.

In his 20 Questions Dustin told me that he and Rahul (the groom) used to build and race toy cars. That was all he gave me. Nothing special, really pretty commonplace. Most little boys play with toy cars—much to the chagrin of today's über-progressive parenting coalition—and lingering on that banal a recollection wouldn't typically offer much to an audience thirsty for originality and humor. But it's always worth wondering how your past recollections impact what you know about the present.

This might sound familiar. This is why I pushed Sherri to summon the Greenwich observatory memory. It's why I asked George about high school and he revisited his cycling shorts. And Eli with his bonsai tree. Hoping there might be more to know with Dustin too, I followed up and asked him to describe the ritual. Where did they get the cars? What happened when they raced? Who usually won? Who was more competitive? Questions, questions. Dig, dig, dig!

To my delight, my hunch had been right and there was more to Dustin's memory of toy cars than their size. There was a delicious metaphor about endurance that was made all the more satisfying by the fact that the thrust of the speech was about how Rahul had grown into an adrenaline junkie with boundless energy and lunatic ideas. In adulthood he was the opposite of slow and steady, so Dustin's initial nostalgia about the cars served as a setup to this contradiction.

> *I've known Rahul for a long time, and for as long as I can remember, he's been a planner and a strategic thinker. The thing we most loved back in those days was to build and play with remote control cars. I would build the fastest car with the biggest engine even if the power ultimately broke the car. Rahul, though, built a far more balanced vehicle. He didn't care about power or speed or fancy wheels. His car was steady and built to endure.*
>
> *This careful and measured approach might not surprise anyone who's been in a car with Rahul at the wheel. He drives like my granny. But it might surprise those of you who know his torpedo-like energy and volume.*

Everything about Rahul is loud: he talks loudly, he laughs loudly, his ideas seem loud somehow—even his clothes are loud. And if you don't believe me because he looks dapper in his tux tonight, just wait till he puts this on. [Here he pulled out a headband] You didn't think I'd let you party without your lime-green headband, did you?

This theme came full circle toward the conclusion as we described Rahul and his fiancée, Beth, as a couple who, in spite of Rahul's high-octane personality, were in fact "just like Rahul's favorite car in high school, the Subaru WRX STI: built to last."

It was pretty damn poetic. And funny. Which is exactly how a wedding speech should end.

Dustin's speech was full of Things That Happen like the toy car racing and other tidbits of anecdotal material that I was able to use by being flexible and open-minded and constantly asking myself, *Why am I using this?* And the sum of all the parts was a very poignant and witty speech with a strong framework bookended by the cars. Even without a singular amazing story, the speech landed a sentimental punch—with humor too.

Some people do have what seems like a big, soaring, naturally occurring perfect story: the mountaineer who nearly died summiting, the scientist who discovered a new microbe, the entrepreneur who built the era-defining tech platform. The story is usually the reason they've been asked to speak in the first place. Even so, these people have to work that much harder to identify the reason they're telling the story and find a way to imbue it with meaning beyond what the audience already knows about them.

I had the precious opportunity to consider how to use a survival story in a speech when a gold-medal-winning Paralympian asked me for help. As an obsessive runner and all-round activity goon, I'm awestruck by stories of triumph over physical disability, but up until that moment I'd never worked with someone who could speak to that experience firsthand.

Connor is a double amputee and is hailed as the world's most skilled player of all time in his sport. During our very first meeting he told me: "Sometimes when I'm wheeling around New York City, someone will walk by me, smile at me knowingly, and thank me for my service. I'm never sure if they'd be more disappointed to know I'm a civilian or that I'm a Canadian." That line! I knew right then this was going to be one of those unforgettable projects. He was comfortable talking about people's misplaced expectations and had a dry, sarcastic wit. I used that line as the first in his speech.

Connor arrived at our office in his wheelchair, which, he explained, he used most of the time. I found him immediately open and easy to talk to. He told me he was looking for someone who could "coach" him or help him work out his messaging. He did not necessarily want someone to take the reins and recast the story he was used to telling word for word. But I assured him that my methodology would allow him to explore his story differently and present it for a new audience. I wanted to make sure that he was going to use such an inspiring back story wisely and to the greatest impact.

In a nutshell, Connor's story went like this.

Like many young Canadian kids growing up in suburbia,

all Connor wanted to be was a pro hockey player. Then one day his best friend's mother and her drunk boyfriend pulled into their driveway, where Connor and his friend were playing. The couple were arguing, and in a moment of rage, the boyfriend hit the gas instead of the brake, sending the car careening into the garage wall right where Connor was standing. The car pinned him to the wall and crushed his legs and in that split second, becoming a pro hockey player became an unattainable dream. As he worked through his loss, however, he began playing wheelchair sports. And today, with multiple gold medals under his belt, he is an icon to many disabled players.

Connor used the story often in talking to kids in middle and high school to drive home messages about the importance of not quitting and the benefits of teamwork. He'd come to me because his latest invitation would put him before a decidedly more sophisticated crowd. The head of a Silicon Valley tech firm, who saw Connor as a model of courage and determination, believed that the company's millennial staffers needed a dose of reality and a lesson in what it means to really work hard. Connor would be speaking to "kids," as they put it, just not quite the kind he was used to addressing.

I've heard a lot of incredible stories, but Connor's account was a moving tale of vulnerability, perseverance, and pragmatism unlike anything I'd ever heard. Still, I was concerned that a blow-by-blow account of the horrors of his accident might unintentionally lead the audience to despair. I love it when people cry listening to speeches, but only if they are tears of inspiration sadness. And the host had been clear she was looking for a speech that would inspire and motivate. So we decided to disrupt the audience's preconceptions about his story at every possible twist. When Connor told the audience about the boy whose dreams were stolen that day, he revealed that he was talking not about himself but about his best friend, whose mother ended up going through the court system and rehab, whose only father figure went to jail, and who himself ended up in the foster care system, penniless and alone. When he told his audience about the morning he woke up in the hospital with no legs, he described his birthday three days later as the best day of his life because he'd never been given so many presents. And then when he recalled the day he sat on a swing and asked God to please show him a sign that he'd get his legs back, we described it as a pivotal moment, because when nothing happened, he realized that his body would be this way for the rest of his life. He was still so young, and yet he was forced to find the maturity that would allow him to accept his fate. It was this moment above all others that changed his life. Not the accident, not the hospital, but a moment quietly swinging alone in his backyard.

We continued to find and link these moments in his life—including how he first got to know his wife—and the wisdom learned from them to experiences the audience might perhaps be able to relate to. For example: Success is having the ability to make choices. Success isn't about how good you are but about how much you are willing to improve. Success isn't an outcome, it's a process.

Let me tell you about my wife for a second. She's super hot. Definitely my biggest victory so far. And she's got legs long enough for both of us. The first time we really talked was at a mutual friend's wedding. I was playing in the band and she came over to say hi while I was tinkering on the piano because she didn't know many people there. And we never stopped talking. The next day it turned out we were both driving to Vancouver alone, so we caravanned all the way. For three days. Canada is huge. Just an FYI for anyone planning on moving there in January. We'd drive one ahead of the other and then stop for gas or lunch at a diner or an overnight stop at a motel. When we got back in our respective cars after each break, we thought about the conversation we'd just had. It was an amazing way to get to know someone. After that trip I moved from Vancouver to New York to study music at Hunter and be closer to her. If you'd asked me at eleven years old what success looked like, I would have said walking to school with my prosthetics. If you asked me at seventeen, I would have told you winning a gold medal for Canada. At twenty-nine? All I wanted to do was write music and be with Mandy.

Left to craft the speech alone, Connor likely would have focused on the main event—namely, his accident and how many medals he won in spite of it—and zeroed in on it as the only story of value. He would have missed telling the audience about how he used to try to outdo his elementary school nemesis, Pete McLaughlin, on the playground by doing more push-ups, and how he would fail every time because of poor form. And as a result he would have missed the callback joke later when he talked about how the coach at his first disabled athletics camp told him he could be the best if he wanted it (and "Pete McLaughlin could suck it"). He wouldn't have known how to include all the other stories about meeting his wife and their road trips together, going to music school, having a baby, and learning to make great pasta. He wouldn't have necessarily known how to make all that relevant to his audience.

When you have a big story like Connor's that people tend to digest as a sort of secular parable, it can be hard to identify other ways of sharing it. But his story is hardly at an end. Connor is only thirtysomething and has his whole life ahead of him. The thing that others understand as being his story is really just a collection of Things That Happened, terrible and wonderful in equal measure. So the thing he needed to do for this speech was to find a way to deconstruct the sequential "once upon a time" framework his audience had inadvertently constructed on his behalf—the one about the boy who lost his legs and became an Olympian—and construct a new narrative around the Things That Happened. We took the story and broke it into pieces. To go back to the why of the story, Connor was in Silicon Valley to draw conclusions, not just to inspire but to teach his audience something. And it worked. Connor emailed afterward to tell me he'd been nervous but way less so than normal, and the speech had been a success. "The power of preparation . . . and good writing," he wrote.

I won't say I've never written a speech and left a story intact; that would be a lie, of course. But it's not often that the story amounts to the speech itself. I can think of only one instance where this was the case, and it was a unique situation.

Adrianne and I were working on our third collaboration when she told me about her sexual assault. I was speechless. I had helped her celebrate the first year of her women's activism group the year prior, and more recently we'd collaborated on talking points for a panel during a highly publicized women's conference in New York City, in which she described how discrimination she'd faced at work had nearly cost the life of her newborn baby. We'd met and chatted at female co-working spaces all over the city, enjoying the common ground we shared as working mothers and women with a desire to help other people. I thought I knew all her big secrets.

She came to me with this revelation just after the Brett Kavanaugh confirmation hearing, when a lot of people were still reeling from the Supreme Court nominee's aggressive self-defense against Dr. Christine Blasey Ford's accusation of sexual assault and the hashtag #WhyIDidntReportIt had emerged on Twitter as a fierce backlash to the men who kept saying, "Well, if this happened, why didn't you report it?'

"When I was sixteen I was raped," Adrianne said very matter-of-factly one day when we were chatting on the phone. Since I say "sorry" about everything, I'm pretty sure that in this moment, when it was actually appropriate, I rose to the occasion, albeit in a sputtering fashion. Adrianne told me that only her husband, parents, and sisters knew. Now she wanted my help in sharing it publicly.

As you know by now, when starting a new project I typically begin with a pragmatic chat aimed at eliciting goals and expectations. Then I think about the questions I might ask to extract original stories that might help shape and color in the message. But with Adrianne I just asked very gently, "Can you tell me what happened?" And for the next twenty-five minutes, while I sat in my office with the banality of everyday business surrounding me, she told me in graphic detail the events leading up to the night of the assault, the moment itself, and the events that followed. It was one of the more upsetting moments of a career spent listening to other people's stories.

Adrianne felt obliged to come forward with her story because of those who responded to Dr. Ford's allegation during the Kavanaugh confirmation hearing by throwing her memory into doubt and pointing to the fact that Dr. Ford had never told the authorities about the assault. When Adrianne was assaulted, she did report it, but the police hadn't believed her; more troublingly, her parents hadn't come to her defense. She wanted to decry the climate of sexism, secrecy, and fear that had ruined lives and caused irreparable harm to people damaged by terrible abuses. If that meant telling everyone what had happened to her, then so be it. She would host a rally in Washington Square Park and invite guests and passersby into the conversation.

Every folder for every speech that every client does is guaranteed to have three documents in it (along with a handful of drafts): notes from the Creative Call, 20 Questions, and the answers to those questions. In this folder, however, there are notes from the call and two drafts. When Adrianne came to the end of the account I realized I didn't need to ask her any questions. Sharing the whole story was the entire point. And doing anything too clever with it would have squandered its raw, authentic power. But it did need a takeaway or a call to action. The point of confessing this atrocity was to highlight the denial and disbelief she'd faced from those who were supposed to protect and defend her. So we punctuated the otherwise unaltered recounting of the story at different moments with the refrain "Can you believe that?"—and we used it about simple, mundane details, like the fact that she went to the vending machine in a hotel unchaperoned at the age of sixteen. As the story became more and more uncomfortable, we kept asking "Can you believe that?" until we forced the audience to decide at what point Adrianne's account of what happened to her had become unbelievable, as it had to the police who took her statement. By the end, the takeaway was very clear: it demanded of the audience at large that you "believe us so that when we report it, you support it." It was a very powerful and very honest unburdening of a lifelong secret—and a good example of how the question "Why am I using this story?" is so important and how any preconceived rules surrounding speech composition are so incredibly limiting.

Aristotle talked about pathos and left it up to the speaker to figure out how to provoke emotion in one's audience. But recently I've been more taken with a much older account of humankind's ability to communicate persuasively. As I alluded to earlier, in his 2018 book *Sapiens,* the Israeli historian Yuval Noah Harari posits the idea that in the wake of what he calls the "Cognitive Revolution," the emergence of the ability to create fiction was what ultimately secured the survival of *Homo sapiens* over all the other species in the *Homo* genus. Their ability to gossip about each other helped them form larger bands of 100 to 150 members, but to create armies and empires they needed another way, and that turned out to be convincing each other to believe in common myths or fictions that enabled them to cross the threshold. Harari suggests that, just as two Catholics will unite around their religion's common myths, two Americans who don't know each other will fight together because they're bonded by their belief in their national myth, and two lawyers will argue together in court to defend a stranger because both believe in laws, justice, and human rights. There is something so powerful to me about Harari's idea that people will come together to organize around ideas, like brands and religions and institutions, simply because of our ability to create imagined realities. When I think of speeches, sure I think about campfires and storytellers, the Greek forum and cave paintings. But I also think about *Homo sapiens* and their imagined realities. I think about how, as speakers, our job is to use our imaginations in the same way our ancient hirsute ancestors did: to employ our stories of amputation, near misses, endurance, survival, and lost passports in creative, unexpected ways.

A story doesn't make a great speech, nor does a speech rely on one great story. But the potential of our anecdotal material can be endlessly exciting if we take the time to examine it, turn it on its head, pick it apart, and then repurpose it by attaching it to stirring data, outlandish truths, and forthright opinions.

PART FOUR
The Polish

9

Get Me TED

The Misconceptions
of Extemporaneity

About a year after my life-changing minivan ride down I-95, a very old friend's grandmother passed away. It was sad, as these stories tend to be, all the more so for the loss of such an ebullient force of nature. As Diane's age had ticked up, her cleavage-baring necklines had dropped lower and the stilettos on which her tiny four-foot-one-inch frame teetered had gotten higher. She could play both the warm and sweet granny and the brassy, sassy broad all at once. She was what my own grandmother would call "priceless." And my grandmother is one to talk. We all loved Diane, especially her grandson. But—and I can't remember if he told me as we walked into the synagogue or whether it dawned on me as he started to speak—at some point it became clear that his plan was to wing the entire speech. His beloved grandmother, whom he'd visited every day, cared for, and confided in, was dead, and he was about to squander the one chance he had to pay tribute to her. And to what end? I have a faint memory of him saying that he didn't feel he needed to write anything down, that he knew her so well he wanted to just "speak from the heart."

I *hate* this saying. It's utterly misleading, because it implies that to do otherwise is inauthentic. I think "speaking from the heart" reveals hubris more than authenticity. At The Oratory Laboratory I like to say we think from the heart and speak from the head. In other words, we rely on the filter of the brain to ensure that our most genuine thoughts, feelings, and ideas are crafted and communicated in a way that guarantees comprehension and engagement. To speak without preparation is to diminish the importance of reaching your audience, and if they aren't compelled by what you say, then why bother at all?

Roughly a year after cringing as I watched my friend stagger between one half-baked thought about his grandmother and the next, I delivered a eulogy of my own as friends and family sat shiva for my much-loved grandfather in Glasgow. Receiving news of his death, I drove straight to JFK, caught a flight from NYC to London to Glasgow, and gave the remarks the following evening. Jews bury their deceased immediately, which isn't great for high-quality eulogies. You might say that my methodology is decidedly un-Jewish in nature, given my emphasis on thoughtful preparation, but it wouldn't be the first time I've been a bad Jew—just ask my grandmother about the time I asked her for more ham when I meant to say tongue. Oh boy. Honestly, I think the crime was being fed tongue. I was clearly too young to stick up for myself.

But I would argue that you can use this methodology on a tight turnaround. I've written plenty of speeches for other people within a twenty-four-hour window. It just requires stimulants. And I would challenge anyone who might accuse my speech of lacking in sincerity and genuine emotion because I spent the transatlantic crossing, the cab ride, and the evening tucked in bed in a weird Airbnb next door to my grandmother's house drafting and redrafting my words.

When I worked on a eulogy to be given by family members of one of the children killed in the Newtown massacre, I can guarantee you that every word on the page came from their broken hearts. They could barely piece together words in real time to respond to friends or reporters, let alone try to piece together a farewell to their five-year-old angel who they'd waved goodbye to on the school bus for the last time days earlier. To think that they'd be able to stand by her grave and string a sentence together in suitable tribute without having first committed their thoughts to paper is outrageous if you ask me. And arrogant. I'm getting all flustered just thinking about it.

The battle for authenticity is one I wage quite often. During the early days of The Oratory Laboratory I fought it on two fronts. First, because a few (and I think quite silly) people accused me of helping people cheat. They believed that asking for help in crafting a speech—especially one that's personal or about someone important—was somehow inappropriate and unsporting. As if gathering and articulating one's thoughts with clarity, intelligence, sentiment, and wit amounted to some kind of competition. This is a ludicrous, old-fashioned, and selfish assessment. And it's perfectly made fun of in the movie *Bridesmaids* when two rival friends of the bride, played by Kristin Wiig and Rose Byrne, enter into a toast battle at the rehearsal night drinks, determined to prove each is the better friend. It's like 8 *Mile* (another great movie) but there's no Eminem, no Mekhi Phifer, and very little lyrical skill involved. When, after going back and forth a few times, Byrne's hostess with the mostest quotes an old Thai proverb, Wiig's jealous maid of honor grabs the microphone back and responds: "Lillian and I took Spanish in school together and so I would just like to say to you and everyone here: gracias para vivar en la casa, en la escuelas and el azul marcada, tienes con bibir en las fochtwaza." The lesson here? Don't ad lib in English. Don't ad lib in a language you don't speak. But do watch *Bridesmaids* if you haven't. You'll thank me.

More commonly, and more often than I'd like, the subject of authenticity comes up with clients who aren't so conflicted about who crafts the language—they're smart enough to know the value in getting help. Instead they suffer from a dilemma of optics. They want their speech to come across as natural and effortless, as if they're just having these wonderfully profound thoughts and revelations in the moment. They want to be Misty Copeland gliding across the stage as the Firebird or Michael Jordan flying through the air to make The Shot. But they forget that anything that looks effortless takes great effort, years of practice, and improvement. So when a client uses the *e*-word I shiver. No, not "effortless." Much worse: "extemporaneous."

One of the reasons the word "extemporaneous" drives me bonkers is because no one who uses it in conversation with me seems to even know what it means. You only have to look it up in a dictionary to understand the confusion, given that there are two definitions and that they lie completely at odds with each other. The first is "composed, performed, or uttered on the spur of the moment," and the second is "carefully prepared but delivered without notes or text." That's not all—in America there is a weird high school debate culture built around a third definition. But let's just deal with the first one first.

The word "extemporaneous" comes from Latin *ex tempore,* which basically means "out of the occasion or time"—in other words, "immediately." According to Merriam-Webster, it was used as early as the seventeenth century to describe spontaneous speech. To be a natural raconteur able to say something intelligent, funny, and poignant on the spur of the moment is to possess a unique skill. Few people are able to pull off this feat. Even Britain's most loved and loathed politician, Boris Johnson, who is famous for his "oopsy-daisy, look at my disheveled hair, I have no idea what I'm doing here, I'm just naturally eloquent" pens his remarks first. And objectively speaking, he's an undeniably effective speaker. The rest of us are average at best. And you're probably one of those, since you're reading this book. There's no shame in that. I'm not particularly good at speaking on the spot without warning. At my Fred Savage birthday bonanza I did feel it was necessary to respond to the speech Nathan delivered, so I slipped into the bathroom and wrote a few notes on a slip of toilet paper. In the time it took to pee I had figured out what I was going to say, but I needed that moment alone. I find bathrooms are the backdrop for many of my best ideas—if there is only one thing you take away from this book, let it be to try hanging out in yours more often.

So "extemporaneity" was synonymous with "spontaneity." Then at some point we gave ourselves a little slack and rewrote the definition to allow us time to prepare our speeches "carefully" and then pretend we didn't. Now they have the *appearance* of spontaneity and effortlessness, but in reality demand a commitment to intense preparation. I have to ask, can this really be considered authentic?

I don't know at what point the third definition came into being. Seemingly for a long time in high schools across America—and I stress America, because in England I never did anything like this; my snowboarding speech was meticulously prepared over the course of many weeks—there has been a thing called the International Extemporaneous Speech Championships, in which participants in this very odd charade are given three questions around which to craft a speech within thirty minutes. (They call their competitions "international" in the same way Major League Baseball calls its championship the World Series. Everyone on the field—bar members of the singular Canadian team—are most definitely American.) So you do get to prepare, but very specifically and arbitrarily, for half an hour. Hooray—a competition, just like the haters wanted! I can't help but wince at how contrived it all is to watch a bunch of teenagers pacing around the stage lecturing us on foreign policy. Talk about inauthentic. And I doubt any of the speakers who seek my help at The Oratory Laboratory give two hoots about who won the International Extemporaneous Speech Championships of 2017.

But I do know there is one word I hear again and again in relation to the *e*-word. And that's "TED."

I'm often told someone is looking for a TED-style speech when they're not in fact speaking at TED. I then ask the obvious question: "What do you mean by 'TED-style'?" When pressed, usually they answer, "Really good and inspiring."

No one is denying that TED can be a very inspiring platform and that it has given us some wonderfully thought-provoking speeches over the years. But if you stray from the top-rated picks, there are as many abominable TED and TEDx speeches as there are audacious and awe-inspiring ones. No one really cares if the speeches are good or bad, though, because the image of the speaker in the center of that red dot has become representative of such an iconic and powerful brand. I'll be the first to admit that the viewer experience—from the big red lettering of the backdrop to the splishy-splashy sound effect at the beginning of each video—is very attractive. Certainly no one calls me and says "I want a Forbes Women speech." Unless, of course, they're due to speak at a Forbes Women event.

But I think what aspiring speakers most admire about the TED Talkers has nothing to do with content and everything to do with that image of themselves in TED mode. They're seduced by the headset and the open stage. People are total suckers for the idea that a speaker can prowl around the stage, paper and podium free, using refrains such as "So I did this thing . . ." and "So let's pretend . . ." and "Imagine this . . . ," pausing, whispering, and eliciting silent "wows" with their facial gestures. What they don't see is that a TED talk is the culmination of months and months—in some cases a year—of practice in making those rhetorical questions seem casual and the speaker's incredulity genuine. There is a reason acting is a job. Bringing a script to life in a believable way is hard and not everyone can do it. It's unrealistic to expect that just anyone can successfully pull that off even after several months of memorization and practice. And who ever gets that generous a deadline? You're lucky if you get one month. And if you fumble even once, if you look up to the ceiling searching for the next words in the middle of your big dramatic moment, you can kiss authenticity goodbye.

Remember Goldie's TEDx speech at Sing Sing? Well, when we got together for a rehearsal, she had tried for days to memorize the speech. I almost always let a client run a speech through once entirely before giving any notes, but about halfway through Goldie's staccato mumbling and apologies for fumbled words, I had to step in and put us both out of our misery. I suggested she stand still in one spot, freeing her body up to move from the ankles up, and just use her script, looking up when she felt comfortable. What an immediate transformation. An extemporaneous transformation, if you will allow an imprecise play on words. She was instantly returned to herself, able to inject her personality behind the words and connect to the truth of the content. She didn't have to think ahead; she didn't have to fake contemplation as she paced (for that is why we pace—to imply a thoughtful process at hand). She was genuine and unencumbered by the pretense. And now that I've seen the video of her turn in the spotlight too, I have the proof my suggestion worked to her benefit. On the day she spoke at Sing Sing she had transferred her script to notecards that kept her present, on track, and confident in the moments that had become more familiar where she could look up. The crowd laughed loudly throughout and then gave her a standing ovation.

Don't misunderstand me—I'm not saying that memorization is destined for disaster. Derrick, for example, was determined to memorize his TV show pitch for the major studios, and though I tried to convince him it wasn't necessary, his stubbornness paid off. He was applying for a grant to work on his second documentary film and was adamant that the candidates were expected to deliver without a script and with plenty of slides to visually represent their project. They were, after all, filmmakers. We worked for about a month on the pitch to make sure it was tight and covered all the points we needed to include, from his experience in the medium to the need for a spotlight on this particular story. And once we locked in the text, he rehearsed every day for weeks, inviting me to practice sessions hosted by the nonprofit council behind the grant process.

Derrick texted me the night of the event, at which all the bigwigs from HBO to Netflix convened to hear the pitches, and told me he'd won. It was so gratifying to receive a formal acknowledgment that my process and method of collaboration was constructive and fruitful. I've received emails to say how well a speech was received, but few of my clients are competing against other speakers for a monetary reward. (Okay, okay, so sometimes it's a competition.) It was wonderful to know that with practice Derrick had been able to persuade the panelists how passionate he was about his work. When memorization works and the speaker can find the connection to the words, it is of course effective. I just don't think it's tantamount to success.

And what of the teleprompter? If you still believe that holding a script is somehow "performative"—in contrast to the act of performing that script—would you also decry the teleprompter? Of course not. Teleprompters are used by pretty much every one of your favorite speakers at one time or another. They help speakers look directly at the audience while fooling people into forgetting they have their speeches scrolling across the screen verbatim. We know they're there and yet we choose to disregard that fact.

There's no one better with a teleprompter than Barack Obama. Yet when people who are trying to describe to me the kind of speech they want, if they don't say they want a TED-style speech, they often mention the former president and his style of speaking. I recall one chap who, when I inquired as to his personal goals for his speech, told me: "I'm really inspired by all the political stuff that's out there." It was an anniversary speech for his grandparents. So not exactly a campaign rally. I imagined him pounding the air with a clenched fist as he told stories about "Martini Mel and Grandpa G-Dog." Indeed, when it came to the delivery session, there was plenty of unnecessary gravitas and clenching. His granny would be too sloshed to notice how odd it was, I reassured myself.

Obama is without a doubt an exceptional orator, both in how he reworks and edits his speechwriters' material and in his fluid but forceful delivery. But his less-famed talent is in how he uses the teleprompter. During his run for a second term some people were so mad at Obama for how good he was at using it that they criticized him for being unable to speak without one in the debates. But that is a false equivalency. To speak for twenty minutes on a thorny issue to a nation of divided voters when the stakes are high is the sort of thing you do with both precision and patience in unpacking your arguments. To debate is to attack the opponent with short, palatable sound bites that cut out the fat and get right to the point. There is no unpacking. Obama's mistake in the debate setting wasn't that he didn't know what he was saying without the teleprompter; it was that he didn't have the precision he gained from having a well-prepared script on the screen.

If we're talking presidents and teleprompters, I'll say that none of my clients have yet made it their goal to emulate Donald Trump. Trump is an anomaly in the speechwriting world. Partly because he doesn't make speeches at all. He rabble-rouses. Famous for straying off script and leaving the administration scrambling to fix his blunders, he once said that they should outlaw teleprompters for anyone running for president. This was before admitting that they were really quite useful when he realized that as president he'd have to make at least some substantive points in his oratory. Trump feels most at home speaking directly to the crowd, slouched across the podium as he makes unscripted, far-fetched accusations and jokes about his opponents. Audience participation is his strong suit; it's what he thrives on—as I said, he's a rabble-rouser. It was entirely unsurprising that he gathered thousands of people during Covid-19 for his rallies—what would he have done with an empty room and a camera? When asked to deliver something meaningful like a State of the Union address using words on a screen, that was where he became static and wooden. The teleprompter, a device to create connection between audience and speaker, was the very thing in his way. As I said, he's an anomaly—in so many ways.

We have a saying at The Oratory Laboratory: "No one will remember if you read your speech, but everyone will remember if you should have." It's impossible to argue with that. Name one speech you've watched that you loved and then thought, *I wish they'd paced around with a headset while they delivered that.* This is why I always prioritize superior content. To me the most genuine thing is to write a damn good speech, take your script up to the podium as proof you cared enough to prepare something, and then do your best to look your audience in the eye when it feels safe. I will always advocate that holding in your bare-naked hand a tight script with humor and a clever narrative structure is not something to fear but rather something to embrace. I am not a coach; I am a writer. I care first and foremost about words. I've written for people who are coaches themselves but who recognized that they didn't have the tools to craft the story on their own, and that no amount of believing in oneself can replace a strong script. My job is not to psych you up and tell you how to feel about what you're saying. It's to help you figure out what you're saying.

Noah found this concept an impossible pill to swallow at first. Although I'm not sure he thought I was a coach as much as he considered me a very expensive assistant. Noah's net worth numbered in the several hundred millions, and I tell you that not to be brash but because it speaks to the fact that he was used to paid employees saying yes to him. It's not my style to accede to someone if it compromises the quality of the work we're doing together. I remember once having a call with Noah, and afterward a friend sitting at a nearby desk said, "Jeez, are you that blunt with all your clients?" He couldn't believe it.

Noah was perfectly charming, but as we continued to work together it became very clear that he was struggling to relinquish control of this unfamiliar creative process to a woman half his age, especially given that, as he told me proudly, he was so good at speaking off the cuff at work. That damn extemporaneity again. Noah had already spent half our first interview session telling me what he thought I would need to do as the speechwriter and what the challenges would be with an intimate anniversary speech. I told him, "Noah, not everyone I work with hosts their birthday dinners in the private dining room at Le Bernardin, but you're not the first to speak about your wife." Actually, I didn't really say that—I'm not that blunt! But I thought it, all right. He spent the rest of our Creative Kickoff meeting telling me about this brilliant speech he'd seen on the internet of a guy giving a toast who didn't have a script, and that the only way to be natural and not all "stiff" was to learn it by heart.

Noah and I argued (with grace and good humor, I swear) all the way up to the night before the speech. As we worked our way through the questions and the edits, he continued to tell me he thought he should memorize it and that this scripting business was going to feel odd. I kept telling him, "Noah, I promise you, when you pull that piece of paper out of your pocket, your audience will feel two things: relief and then excitement. They'll fill their glasses and get ready for a good old time. And that's just what you'll give them." A close second to Derrick's triumphant text was Noah's message following the party. It read: "Victoria, the speech went great. Everyone loved it. Thank you. I'm a true believer now in the written speech and superior content!"

Like Noah, a lot of people who are routinely called on to present in a work environment confuse experience with ability. I can assure you, reading through PowerPoint slides every day in a conference room does not a legendary speaker make. The most egregious recurring offense committed in the corporate realm is failing to acknowledge that while a slide deck may be an essential component of a presentation, the slides shouldn't tell the story, they should illustrate it. It's been said that *Citizen Kane* is a perfect movie because even on mute you still get the story. The deck you leave behind in a meeting or conference is the *Citizen Kane* version. The deck you use to present live, however—whatever the forum—is far more minimal in exposition. The slides are there to back up your points, set up questions, and draw conclusions, and they should combine thoughtful copy with savvy design.

Minimalism and high design do not come naturally to the corporate crowd, to whom a unifying company logo on every page means that something is "designed." When a leading social media platform called and asked for a bid to work with forty speakers at their annual recruitment conference, I had no idea I'd be giving birth the day of the kickoff. By the time the event rolled around, every day in my life was a challenge to squeeze in as much as I could—whether it was squeezing my bottom into pre-baby clothes for meetings or squeezing in phone calls in between naps and feedings. The speakers I'd been hired to help were breakout speakers—a particularly unfortunate name that always makes me think of acne. Breakout sessions feature not the keynote speakers but the people running the workshops, presentations, and seminars in the peripheral areas of the convention center where there is less gaping in admiration and more note-taking. They make up the second page of the conference pamphlet, and they're usually very ambitious and determined to make a splash in their field.

You might think that the logistics of shepherding forty speakers through a creative process in under two months was challenging enough. Or even that finding originality and excitement in forty presentations about talent recruitment and retention might be close to impossible. But honestly, I have rich and intriguing learnings from writing speeches on subjects one might imagine are relentless in their tedium. Hotel staffing, software development, the car rental industry . . . it's all fascinating stuff, I swear. No, it wasn't the tedium of the subject matter that brought me to the boiling point again and again. And it wasn't hormones. It was instead the jumbled, ugly slide decks that every single speaker presented to us in the Creative Kickoff meetings as evidence that they didn't need our help. Because the speakers were hostile to any suggestion that we might try a more integrated approach with visuals and narrative created in unison, my team and I got to work trying to create narratives around the slides their in-house teams had already assembled. It was a shit show, and with all the diaper changing I was doing around that time, I mean that in all possible definitions.

The issue I take with this "deck first" approach is that the speaker is not really thinking about the story they're telling and the audience experience. They're thinking of data points and pie charts and what chunks of text to put on the slide. I found that on every occasion, even if the presenter knew what the big takeaways were, they hadn't spent any time thinking about how they might set up that message and then pay it off at the end in a meaningful way. They didn't consider the other kind of material they might need to facilitate a meaningful connection with the audience.

Designing a deck for a presentation should be a holistic creative exercise. How to do this successfully could occupy the pages of an entirely separate book—perhaps a sequel; who knows? But what's important here is that they missed the crucial step of sitting down and writing out some form of script, of thinking about how the deck and story complemented each other—what they would open with, what the arc was, and how they would bring it full circle.

At these kinds of events, there is a whole lot of love for the headset and the pacing. But there are so many ways to create superior content and then nail the delivery. You can put a whole script up on speaker notes and use a prompter. You can boil the script down to bullets and practice using one note-card with the key beats of the narrative in your hand. And yes, you can request a podium, keep still, and use your script. If the content is good, no one will care. I know it's not very sexy, but really, are we there to check out your legs or your ideas?

A few years ago at the GLAAD Media Awards the actress Kerry Washington went up to receive an award and discovered there was no podium. Of course! At a glitzy event like that they definitely want to see a bit of leg or gown at the very least. If she was flustered, though, you barely noticed. She held her paper and read her speech about communities on the fringes and marginalized voices in entertainment and media. Reading the speech did not stop her from connecting with the audience, who gave her a raucous ovation. Neither did it stop her from engaging a much larger audience in the subsequent days, as the speech went viral.

I know we're not all Kerry Washington. I know the bone structure and the gown do count for something. But they don't excuse a bad speech. Remember Gwyneth's weepy Oscar bomb? We all have different strengths and weaknesses, but there is a solution for everyone, and I do believe it should always start with a script of superior content—and in most cases end there too. If you've done the work of creating a rich and thrilling narrative and can connect to the words, owning the sentiment, the passion, and the conviction, I promise you no one cares about a piece of paper.

Again, no one will remember if you read your speech, but everyone will remember if you should have. Which camp would you prefer to be in?

10

A Pipe, a Plank, and a Wheelbarrow

Churchill's Key Elements, Revised

In 1897, Winston Churchill—that beloved wizard of public oratory—wrote an essay that was not published until after his death. It was titled "The Scaffolding of Rhetoric," and in it he outlined what he believed to be the five "principal elements" of effective speech:

1. *Correctness of diction*
2. *Rhythm*
3. *Accumulation of argument*
4. *Analogy*
5. *Wildness of language*

Think of this chapter as my version of Churchill's scaffolding. Though a more accurate title might be something closer to "A Pipe, a Plank, and a Wheelbarrow: The Construction Site of Speech." Just as I'm not a scholar on Churchill, I don't possess the credentials to preach a lesson on alliteration and syntax. As I said before, I cannot promise to make you a better writer. I stopped studying English at sixteen, and truthfully, for the better part of my childhood I was hell-bent on the idea that I would one day be a famous film director—my qualification as a teenager was the 60 percent or so of my time spent hanging out in the Prime Time video store around the corner from our family home in London, where, while helping out for free reshelving the videos, I was able to offer unsolicited film reviews to customers. There they were thinking they'd nip in to grab a movie on a Friday night; little did they know they'd be ambushed by a cocky teenager at the counter opining on Tarantino and Spielberg.

I made a fast friend in a kind Serbian movie buff who'd worked at the store for years and finally found I was old enough to talk to. An aspiring filmmaker himself, Goran would cast me as the protagonist in most of the short films he wrote and directed; in fact, it was his championing of me as an actress that eventually drove me to drama school and the short-lived pursuit of a career in acting. Today I like to think I landed squarely in the sweet spot, bang in the middle of all these disciplines. I write for the audience, I interpret for the speaker, and I direct for both. Voilà. It's not exactly Churchillian, but it's how I'm able to help you navigate this big moment when you come to flesh out the draft. And it's how I've determined that the most important objectives when it comes to the act of writing number only three: clarity, authenticity, and originality.

While I wouldn't be so bold as to wholly disregard a titan of the podium as beloved as Churchill—for fear of being canceled by toastmasters the world over—there is plenty about his scaffolding that for me no longer holds up. Not only is the focus on political speeches myopic and his perspective on the people who can make them—namely, men—equally shortsighted, but in society today, one hundred years after Churchill penned his essay, a speaker need not aspire to "correctness of diction" or "wild language" to ensure a re-action from their audience. Placed in any forum today, an orator can instead lean heavily on the synthesis of ideas—the way connections and conclusions are drawn—to provoke, surprise, and move their audience.

It's not the fashion to wow people with an excessive and elaborate vocabulary the way Churchill would have you believe. Of course, it will delight certain people, for whom lexicon is a turn-on, but grammatical acuity and orotund language are neither an expectation nor a requirement for a speech. The words you use are important, of course; it's just that when you sit down to write your speech, it need not be with a dictionary. People genuinely don't care if you went to private school and use Latin derivations. (Even though that's really helpful in understanding words like "extemporaneous"!) And it is wildly unfashionable to even suggest that there is a correct way to speak.

So I will always advocate for the effort of impressing an audience by the poetry of your ideas rather than the poetry of your language. If you've done the work at the Crazy Wall and crafted a solid outline, you can rest assured that your creativity there will compensate for any shortcomings in the linguistic arena.

It's amazing, for example, what a sofa can do to incite an audience to action. Adrianne's first speech with me marked the one-year anniversary of her advocacy group, which came into existence very shortly after Trump took office. Reeling from the polarization and hateful language she saw permeating social media, she began to invite women to a weekly salon to talk about what the hell was going on and how they might be able to get more active in their communities and in society at large. In the very first of her 20 Questions I had asked her what the most upsetting tweet or Facebook post she'd seen had been, and in her answer she told me about an ex-boyfriend of hers from high school who had posted a litany of anti-immigrant propaganda. Adrianne is half Native Hawaiian and half Filipino, so reading his messages rocked her to the very core.

Further down the questionnaire I asked her about the living room in the house back in Texas where she lived with her parents. By doing so, in my mind I was trying to make a connection to the living room setting of her activist group's weekly meetings, but when we dug a little deeper, it transpired that the immaculate living room had been one of the few places Adrianne's father had let her and that very same boyfriend spend time alone when they were dating. Suddenly the living room's role in the speech transformed from a potential joke about plastic-covered sofas to a linchpin in the narrative.

When I was in high school, I dated a boy named Chad. He was a sweet guy. Loved performing. His Garth Brooks impersonation was spectacular. (That's who you impersonate when you're a teenager in small-town Texas.) He was a people pleaser—Chad, not Garth Brooks—the kind of kid who genuinely wanted to do the right thing. And even though he was a really innocent, good-hearted person, my parents still didn't trust us to even hang out in the kids' den because it was too near my bedroom.

A Pipe, a Plank, and a Wheelbarrow

We were confined to the formal living room downstairs, where we weren't allowed to touch anything and the carpet still had stripes from where it had been vacuumed days before. Chad and I talked about anything and everything while we sat there—what fueled our passions, what we'd want to do with our lives, where we'd want to explore. Chad proposed before my eighteenth birthday because, Texas, and even though I said no, we stayed in touch for a bit until losing contact in college. By that time he'd gotten married and had four kids. He never really explored anywhere or left the Bible Belt.

Last year, around the time of the Muslim ban, Chad reentered my life. On Facebook, as all exes eventually do. But when I read his post I didn't hear his goofy Texas lilt singing "Friends in Low Places" anymore. It was an angry, hateful voice spewing a diatribe of anti-Muslim vitriol. "All immigrants," he'd written, "should be detained and questioned before coming to the States."

Hundreds of US visa holders, green card carriers, and vetted refugees at the time had just been told they were no longer welcome in America. My reunion with Chad felt every bit as devoid of warmth. My father is a Muslim who came to New York from the Philippines in the 1970s on political asylum. He is the embodiment of the very person Chad was now saying he wanted out. If my father wasn't here, I wouldn't be here. So I had to wonder, did Chad want me gone too? Try as I might, I couldn't reconcile this character on my news feed with the sweet guy from Texas I remembered sitting on my sofa.

For days, his words rang in my ear. It was like that

feeling you get after a really loud concert, but I didn't have any merch or Instagram likes to show for it. And the more I looked at Facebook and Twitter, the more deafening it all was. We all saw what happened after the election. Facebook turned into the Hunger Games. People on both sides of the aisle preyed on one another's fears and resentments, neighbors turned on each other, political ideals that once didn't matter tore apart friendships. He or she who could shout the loudest won the attention of the media, but only until the next hashtag popped up on Twitter and a new war began.

But it wasn't the white supremacists that scared me. And it wasn't the fact that politicians felt comfortable turning a blind eye to a child molester. It wasn't the Russia probe or the attack on women's rights or the stripping of Obamacare.

What I worried about most was that beyond all the noise on social media, all the cries of Make America Great Again, and all the hear-me-roaring, I heard something else. A deafening silence.

The silence of confusion. The silence of a million unasked questions. The silence of hundreds if not thousands of women like you and me who, regardless of education and social literacy, knew how they felt but hadn't found a place where they felt safe enough to articulate it in a meaningful way.

It's easy to throw up a hashtag and decry a prochoice abortion bill. But what about when you're not so sure about the issue? How many of us are brave enough to speak up and say, "Hey, I don't know everything

*about this"? Because who really knows what the Wom-
en's March was about? How do you talk to your neocon
uncle at Thanksgiving? Or your racist ex-boyfriend, for
that matter? How do you speak up in a debate if you're
not even a US citizen? What should you tell your representative? What is a representative?*

*I felt as if a blanket of quiet was suffocating the im-
pulses, urges, and reactions of so many people. And I
knew that I didn't want to be quiet anymore.*

*So I returned to the living room—to the place I'd
spent so many hours waxing lyrical about my hopes
and dreams with a boy who later prompted so many
questions—and I looked for answers from people who felt
the same way. People like you.*

If you spend as much time watching speeches as I do, you'll
see these powerful moments of connection everywhere. In
Churchill's essay he talks about a "wild extravagance of
language" and quotes as an example some old codger in
politics called Mr. Bryan (he's probably very famous) as saying: "You shall not press a crown of thorns upon the brow of
labor or crucify humanity on a cross of gold." I can see how
that stirred the crowds in 1896. Now? The auditorium would
have just emptied out. (Concessions, anyone?) Nowadays the
"extravagance" is not linguistic as much as it is conceptual.
A modern-day comparison might be Earl Spencer's eulogy
of his sister Diana, Princess of Wales, in which he said:

*It is a point to remember that of all the ironies about Diana,
perhaps the greatest was this—a girl given the name of the*

ancient goddess of hunting was, in the end, the most hunted person of the modern age.

That one gets me every time. I felt the same punch to the gut in 2019 when TV personality Jon Stewart—former host of *The Daily Show*—delivered a very public shaming of members of Congress. He was furious that they still had not provided adequate healthcare and other benefits to the 9/11 first responders who suffered from illnesses as a result of the toxic substances they were exposed to as the towers burned. Halfway through the speech he toned down his anger to pay tribute to their service.

The official FDNY response time to 9/11 was five seconds. Five seconds. That's how long it took for FDNY, for NYPD, for Port Authority, EMS to respond to an urgent need from the public. Five seconds. Hundreds died in an instant. Thousands more poured in to continue to fight for their brothers and sisters.

Stewart then continued for another six heart-wrenching minutes before wrapping it up with this:

Thank God for people like John Feal, thank God for people like Ray Pfeifer, thank God for all these people who will not let it happen. They responded in five seconds. They did their jobs with courage, grace, tenacity, humility. Eighteen years later, do yours.

In those six minutes I had been chewing on my lip in nervous anticipation hoping that he would pay off the "five seconds" line at the close, but I have to say, as someone who is always skeptical of celebrities making political speeches, Stewart really made me eat humble pie that day.

I suspect that some of you might be foaming at the mouth in indignation that I would smite the English language as an integral part of rhetoric, but you can calm down. I work exhaustively with the writers I hire on word choice and grammar. Sometimes I think I drive them crazy with the way I pick apart a sentence and reshuffle the words. It's not because there is anything more complex about writing for speech than there is about writing for the printed page. Quite the opposite. It's that writing for speech has to be so very bare. Many writers wrestle with how un-dressed-up it is. When I'm hiring new writers, I intentionally avoid those whose resumes or samples contain long-form journalism or creative writing. The best writers have always been those who have little experience writing or those who have honed their craft in the area of film scripting. It's tempting to want to work with experienced writers, of course, but the curse is that they're so often unable to achieve the level of clarity a live audience needs.

But you don't have me looking over your shoulder needling you about the way you construct your sentences. So I'll tell you that the biggest mistake an aspiring writer will make is to overuse adjectives and adverbs, allowing them to do the work that nouns and verbs should do. This, and using the passive voice instead of the active. I hope it is sufficient to say that I'm not suggesting a writer strike these elements from their work completely; that would be madness. But as Voltaire once wrote: "The adjective is the enemy of the noun." So too, Stephen King once wrote: "The road to hell is paved with adverbs." With so many creepy horror novels under his belt, he should know. The writer and professor Ben Yagoda described the common habit of using descriptors this way in a 2007 *New York Times* piece:

> *The root of the problem is lazy writers' inordinate fondness for this part of speech. They start hurling the epithets when they haven't provided enough data—specific nouns and active verbs—to get their idea across. It's easy—too easy—to describe a woman as "beautiful." It takes more heavy verbal lifting, but is more effective, to point out that the jaw of every male in the room dropped when she walked in. And establishing that someone kicked an opponent who was down, stole seventeen dollars from a Salvation Army collection kettle, and lied to partners about having sexually transmitted diseases precludes the need to call him terrible, awful, horrible, horrid, deplorable, despicable, or vile.*

In speech especially this holds true. Consider the following story told in a wedding speech. The setting is a family home in the evening. The narrator is describing the moment in which her new son-in-law—a football-playing physical giant—returned home unexpectedly early from months away, wanting to surprise his girlfriend (now his wife). She was upstairs; the rest of the family were downstairs, watching in excitement and anticipation.

> *Despite his ungainly six-foot-seven frame, Kevin crept upstairs stealthily and silently, leaping over every creaky stair,*

as we lingered at the foot of our ancient, rickety staircase, both highly entertained and admiring of his balletic impulses.

I've had writers and speakers alike who would have lapped up such a verbose account, but now read that aloud. It's far too frilly and pretentious. Audiences do not get to reread a paragraph; they only get one shot to hear and make sense of what you're saying. So phrasing and word choice are both vital to consider. When I read my own drafts I always do so aloud and ask myself whether the idea in any one sentence is easy to grasp. I want to make sure the audience can follow the logic throughout. Even when you're alone, it's pretty easy to tell instinctively whether something is confusing or rambling (or merely boring). You just have to be honest as soon as you suspect that's the case and work humbly to fix it. The writing must be simple and straightforward, and yet with it you have to paint a vivid picture to keep the audience engaged and invested. I will say to writers in training: "Be simple, but be very specific and thoughtful about what you do with the plain language. Stop trying to 'write' it and instead think about how to talk about it."

This is a closer approximation to how the narrator could retell this story for a live crowd:

So there we all were, watching from below as Kevin climbed the stairs to Sofia's room, carefully dodging the creakiest steps—you know our house is very old. I guess after years of overnight stays he knew exactly which those steps were, because the way he leapt and pirouetted around them, it was like watching Alvin Ailey perform in Revelations. *I was just sorry I was wearing sweatpants and a kitchen apron. If I'd known, I would have dressed up for the show.*

If the point is to entertain the crowd with the image of this hulking linebacker advancing so daintily, then you have to take pains to paint that picture. The language is far more straightforward in the second version, and in place of the adjectives are verbs to describe the action as well as a simile to describe the reaction of the witnesses at the bottom of the stairs.

Churchill was maddeningly ambiguous on the kind of language a good speaker should employ. He both reveled in the exactness of adjectives, which implies a strong command of the English language, and simultaneously encouraged the use of short, "Anglo-Saxon" words of "common, homely usage." During a lecture on his predecessor, Boris Johnson (yes, the very same flimsy-haired Brexiteer from earlier) pointed out that Churchill's skill was being able to maneuver so deftly between the two modes. He uses as his example Churchill's line "Never in the field of human conflict was so much owed by so many to so few." The first half of the sentence is "pompous and bombastic," explained Johnson. After all, Churchill just meant "never in war." But then the abruptness of what follows—"so much," "so many," "so few"—packs a powerful punch made even stronger by its juxtaposition with the florid prose that precedes it. To add to this, it's a nice triplet—a lyrical trick we should all keep up our sleeves, since it is long established that people absorb information in sets of three.

While Churchill and I might disagree on using flowery adjectives and bombastic verbiage in place of a richer and more visual description, we do agree that simplicity wins the day and that in the quest for emotional appeal, rhetorical devices such as similes, analogies, and metaphors are handy weapons in a speechwriter's arsenal. As Churchill puts it: "[An analogy] appeals to the everyday knowledge of the hearer and invites him to decide the problems that have baffled his powers of reason by the standard of the nursery and the heart."

Think back to Alex's speech about his brother and how that tagline helped frame the loss of their father and the groom's maturity. Or recall Rebecca's speech at the equine therapy school graduation ceremony. In that speech Rebecca used her daughter's gifts on the snowboard to talk about how while Izzy had what snowboarders call enviable "lift," which propelled her to stardom in the community, the confidence it took to get such lift created a blind spot for her back on the ground. She spoke of the false sense of security Izzy had and her inability to recognize that she had a problem. "Her confidence on the board," we wrote, "I think deceived *her*." At the end of the speech Rebecca used the metaphor of lift and the blind spot to describe Izzy's transformation and her future:

> *You've always had amazing lift, and now you have the gift of perspective and clear sight. I look forward to watching you make this the most awesome 180 anyone has ever seen.*

Clarity extends beyond just the words you choose. It's also in the words you choose not to use, as well as in the punctuation between words. Since Churchill didn't necessarily put pen to paper when he crafted his speeches, he would rarely have had to consider what the script looked like and how to bring it to life. He wrote a lot of his speeches in real time with an assistant to transcribe his thoughts as he paced around his office. You might say his process was the reverse of the one I describe in this book. I've tried Churchill's method—while writing this book, in fact, thanks to a bout of tendinopathy and the inconceivable pain in my hand that made it impossible to even hold my hand to the keyboard. I tried using voice notes with a transcription app—because of course Churchill had an iPhone. But I found I couldn't make the connection that way. I think as I write. Some people speak as they think. As a result, I took some handwritten notes, and then, while my wrist and hand healed, I turned my attention to a bit of home improvement. I fell behind on the writing but threw out an ugly Ikea bookcase I'd had since 2006. There's a silver lining when you know where to look.

One of the wondrous gifts of writing for speech is that you don't always need to make a smooth transition between paragraphs and the ideas contained within them. This is not the case in book writing, as I myself learned from my editor's notes. If I had to pick one thing that held me back or tripped me up as I was writing this book, it wouldn't be the constant interruption by a child wandering into the office to say nothing of any consequence; it would be that I struggled to make the transitions. In speech you have every right to change the subject when you want as long as you signal this in your delivery.

I'll use some remarks I scripted for Jenna Bush Hager as an example. In setting up the final call to action, I wanted to use something that her grandfather President George H. W. Bush had said.

It's still hard to believe that COPD is the third-leading cause of death. It kills more people than diabetes and more than liver disease. And while 30 million people in America suffer from some form of it, it is woefully underfunded, receiving less than cancer, diabetes, or Alzheimer's. With biomass fuels, vaping, and genetic predisposition undiagnosed in families worldwide, we are heading towards a bleak future of suffering and unnecessary loss.

My grandfather George Herbert Walker Bush hated the word "legacy." When people asked him what he wanted his legacy to be, it bothered him immensely. He resented the idea that the things we might be doing or thinking about tomorrow were more important than what we were doing right now, in the present.

We already know what the future of COPD looks like. It's what happens today that matters.

In this excerpt, "my grandfather" may seem on the page like a non sequitur after "unnecessary loss," but with the right pause in the delivery it would effectively signal the beginning of her conclusion that now is the time for action. As it turned out, Hager, now a co-host of the *Today* show, nailed the pause but then strayed from the script, adding a lot of fluff in the "legacy" paragraph—which meant that the thread between the future and the legacy and the now was lost. Luckily, this was a video piece, so we saved it in the editing room—another, good reminder to stick to the script!

If you have a tight script, a pause and an infusion of fresh energy do all the work for you. That's why I despise transitional fluff like "anyway" or "just kidding" or "but seriously though." I don't even particularly like "so" at the beginning of a sentence. But that's a style that is popular here in America, and I'm reluctant to be overly sanctimonious about the purity of an ever-evolving language, especially in the oral tradition. What irks me about "anyway," "but seriously though," and other such inane fillers is how apologetic they sound, especially after a joke. It's as if the speaker is somehow embarrassed by what came before or what is coming next. I've been told a million times before that these transitions make the speaker come across as more conversational and authentic, but a speech isn't as casual as a conversation. Which brings me to my next point. (Breath. Transition.)

Being this casual does not make you sound more natural and authentic, despite what you may believe. But where I previously shooed away the notion of authenticity in terms of whether you use a script during your speech, when it comes to your voice—what you say and how you say it—I'm all in.

A certain type of person might have raised an eyebrow while reading this line from Adrianne's excerpt above: "Chad proposed before my eighteenth birthday because, Texas." My parents would have for sure. My friends back in London wouldn't have raised an eyebrow but might have squinted in confusion. If I were writing that line for, say, Noah, I would have written "because that's what you do in Texas." But I knew that Adrianne, being just on the borderline between the millennials and Gen X, would definitely pull off the slang, and the crowd at the event would take it with a hint of tongue in cheek. A boomer wouldn't have gotten the humor, and if I had included that in Noah's speech in an attempt to be cool, it would have sounded ridiculous. You might think this is obvious, but speakers often hope to ingratiate themselves with the audience by using language that isn't appropriate or authentic, either because it's too colloquial or it's too grandiose. It reminds me of how my mother used to coo about something being "wicked" just to impress my teenage friends. So embarrassing!

I learned this lesson early on while working with Sandra, although in her case the mismatch was completely my fault. When I started writing speeches for other people I knew I had to figure out how to adapt my native writing voice—long sentences, sarcasm, Anglicisms like "ice lolly," "tweeny," and "boot"—into a more neutral voice. As I fought with these issues, Sandra emailed me from Florida asking me to help her with a speech at her son's wedding. During the early iterations of our process we didn't speak to the client before the delivery session—everything was conducted electronically. This seems now like a terrible plan for a speechwriting company, but at the time this was all new and we were just making it up as we went along.

Sandra liked the speech I wrote for her and her edits were minimal, so everything seemed to be going swimmingly—until I got on the phone with her for the delivery session and discovered to my amazement that when she had told me her family was originally from Cuba, by "originally" she meant last year! Her English was that of an advanced beginner, to be generous, and she spoke with a thick accent, stumbling over the phrasing and all the words she clearly didn't know yet. I stopped her and gently suggested a rewrite that would better suit her fluency and cadence. With a bit of back-and-forth, together we prevailed.

I know you know if you're a non-English-speaking Cuban or not, but you still need to make sure that the words you pick and the references you make feel and sound natural—or, if not, that you acknowledge the incongruity.

One of my most effervescent collaborators is a leading medical expert in his field who originally hails from Mumbai. When reading the first draft of a speech he would be delivering at a family party, he got to the section where he mentioned his wife, and then asked me with a quizzical look on his face: "Victoria, what does this mean: 'she carried me when I needed support'?" I explained that my intention was to acknowledge that she had been the family's breadwinner when he was a lowly intern. He burst out laughing and told me that his Indian audience was very literal-minded, and would in that moment imagine his wife picking him up and physically carrying him.

Anil also told me, however, that he wanted to explain to his guests that the reason he was hosting this family party was he wanted his grandchildren to be able to "go down to the basement when they're older and flip on the DVD player years later to see the kind of grandfather they had." Now it was my turn to laugh. I told him, "Anil, no one uses DVDs anymore. In twenty years they'll be watching this in augmented reality." It just so happened that his eldest son was a tech venture capitalist. So we preserved the integrity of his original wish with a reference to dusty DVDs in the basement, and then made a fun nod to his authentic lack of technical prowess by adding an offhand quip: "I know, I know, Ajay is shaking his head. Don't worry, Ajay, I'll store it on the Apple TV too."

We didn't want to make a joke that was too tech-savvy because it would have come off as suspiciously inauthentic. But Apple TV was a believable reference. Granted, if Anil had been writing the speech himself, no great harm would have been done by excluding the joke (save for a few giggles at his expense from anyone in the room who was under sixty), but it shows the nuances of authenticity.

As you deliberate on the exact words to express yourself, consider that the authenticity is not static but a moving target. In one forum you might want to keep the language looser and more conversational. In another you might want to be more formal and elevated. With one audience you might curse if it feels appropriate; with another, not in a million years. When activist Tamika Mallory stood on the street after the death of George Floyd, her cries to the government of "Dammit, you do better" were piercing. When the students at Marjory Stoneman Douglas High School chanted, "We call BS," the teenage rallying cry ricocheted through the gun control debate community around the country. But in either case, in a different environment with a different audience, the language might well not have been as forceful. This doesn't make either choice more or less authentic.

Clients distracted by concerns of authenticity often ask how I'll capture their voice. But it can be misleading to assume you even know what your voice is as it pertains to public speaking, because speech is an elevated form of communication. Your voice at the poker table on Friday nights is likely not the voice with which you tell your kids to get back into bed, and very unlikely to be the same with which you introduce yourself to your new employees at an orientation breakfast.

When I work with clients I am hyperaware of their verbal rhythms and cadence, age, gender, and cultural background, because all those factors affect the way they speak. But I also have to convince people that there is a difference between how you might chat to someone in a bar and how you speak to an audience in an auditorium or on video; that there is a contrast between how you write and how you speak; and that there is a difference between how we express ourselves privately to an individual and publicly to a group. Kanye West once told David Letterman in an interview that he loves people "being the maximum versions of themselves." As someone who thinks a lot about how we present ourselves, that struck me. I honestly think we're too complex for that to make sense. Aren't we always conditioned by the context and people in it?

I tried to explain this as simply as I could to Dee, who wanted to craft a toast for a close friend who, I was tickled to learn, happens to be one of the biggest superstars of our day. The venue for Dee's remarks was an intimate dinner of twelve people at his home to celebrate his birthday, and her objective, she explained to me, was just to tell him how special he was to her. I had twenty-four hours to get it turned around, knowing nothing and with no brief.

She'd written to him over the years and offered to send me some of her emails so I could get a sense of their relationship and the way she spoke to him. I can't lie—I was more than curious to see these and through them understand a little more about this entrepreneurial goliath. Talk about private jokes—this was a private language. Metaphors were confused and mismatched, sentences lacking in punctuation left me clueless as to their meaning, and private terms of affection were mystifying. At 3:00 a.m., I had given up reading and was trying to write an email that honored Dee's willingness to reveal herself to me but that gently persuaded her to try something different for the speech.

While it's not my job to judge how people communicate

privately, I do have to try to make sure that in a more public-facing forum those authentic traits of self-expression are tempered by a more ubiquitous style of elocution. I had to explain to Dee that a private email intended for a best friend is *very* different from a piece of writing intended to be delivered out loud in a room with other people. Half-sentences with exclamations of adoration midway through would not sound as poetic as she might have intended in the emails. We needed to translate the emotion and capture her personality while making sure her bestie and his guests actually understood what she was saying as they sipped Châteauneuf-du-Pape and puffed on Cubans. Cigars, not people.

One thing I couldn't have faulted Dee for was falling into the trap of using clichés—her style was definitely idiosyncratic. Then again, there is a reason expressions like "he's my rock" are so popular. They are clear and make sense, unlike much of Dee's writing. But I'll take her unique embellishments over overused tropes any day.

Look, I'll be as clear and practical here as I can. If you find yourself writing something like "it's not a sprint, it's a marathon" but your speech is about the environmental crisis in Tasmania, think about what imagery and anecdotal material you're using and create a new metaphor with the same meaning. If you find yourself writing that someone "needs no introduction," then tell the audience something in the introduction that they don't actually already know about that person. If you find yourself writing "she's my rock," consider she might be something other than a heavy pebble, something more specific and personal. If she works out every day, how about "She's not my rock, she's my twenty-pound free weight"?

Clichés are such a mood killer, if you ask me. And such a disappointment when you've worked so hard and succeeded at giving the crowd something they've never heard before. I'll never forget how disappointed I was with Obama for using the old rock metaphor to describe Michelle—she deserves so much better. Bonnie Fuller, a celebrity editor at *Us Weekly*, wrote about Michelle Obama: "Those arms . . . look powerful enough to wrap around a distressed nation and lift it up." That's more like it!

Clichés are lazy, and writing is not lazy. It's very active. It's your brain and your body working together. To stand any chance of having a productive writing session, you must come to it alert and ready rather than sleepy or reluctant. If you're not in the right headspace, chances are you'll not be productive, so when you do set out to write your speech, it pays to have as much time on your side as possible. There are days when I just instinctively feel disconnected from the material and the desire to tangle with it, so I don't pressure myself, because I know when the mood passes I'll more than make up for the lost time. Some days an early morning session before anyone else is awake and I'm nursing a milky coffee is prime time. Some days I'm bouncing around the room with my desk wound right up to standing height. Some days I listen to music I know so that I can ignore the lyrics; other days I need instrumental music in order to focus. Sometimes I write my best work on a subway commute inspired by the people around me. Sometimes I need to lock myself away from everyone. But always, when I'm stuck the only thing that works is getting up and going for a walk. Being away from your screen and in your head will always get those cranial synapses firing. So be good to yourself and give yourself the permission to stroll.

Churchill ended his "Scaffolding of Rhetoric" this way:

> *Throughout the country are men who speak well and fluently, who devote opportunity, talent and perseverance to improving their speaking and yet never deserve to be called orators. The subtle art of combining the various elements that separately mean nothing and collectively mean so much in an harmonious proportion is known to a very few. Nor can it ever be imparted by them to others. Nature guards her secrets well and stops the mouths of those in whom she confides. But as the Chemist does not despair of ultimately bridging the chasm between the organic and the inorganic and of creating the living microcosm from its primordial elements, so the student of rhetoric may indulge the hope that Nature will finally yield to observation and perseverance, the key to the hearts of men.*

If you read this picturing its author as Britain's portly wartime wordsmith, it would sound pompous and self-serving. But Churchill was only twenty-three when he wrote it. As an orator, he had achieved absolutely nothing at this stage besides a tireless study of other people's speeches in the House of Commons, where his father, Lord Randolph, was Leader. He is not the orator who knows "the subtle art of combining the various elements that separately mean nothing and collectively mean so much in an harmonious proportion." He is the student of rhetoric who is hopeful and persistent. Look what he became. There is hope for all of us!

11

The Room for Laughter

How to Be Funny When You Think You're Not Funny

The joke read: "You're more likely to find wasabi in Saudi Arabia than a Wahhabi. We have some fantastic restaurants in Riyadh if you're ever in town."

I suppose I have to concede that a joke like that on Capitol Hill may have been somewhat . . . I don't know, flippant? After all, this was a speech on counterterrorism that opened with the retelling of an interception of plastic explosives hidden on a flight to Chicago. Perhaps trying to make a bunch of "stiffs in suits" laugh at a political briefing was inappropriate. It wasn't exactly a comedy piece, and I daresay my client needed a lot more than a joke to convince US policymakers that Wahhabism as a formal organization or secular dogma didn't exist. But I couldn't help trying for even a small gag.

You might be wondering how I came to be palling around with a Saudi representative in Washington in the first place, and it is a peculiar story worth retelling. I'd been contacted by a young man who told me he had an important briefing in DC and that he could use my help laying out his arguments, along with all the substantive evidence, in a convincing way.

He had been tasked with persuading the American government that the Saudis were really great allies, trying their hardest to work with the United States in rooting out insurgents in the Middle East. Serious stuff, right?

The first challenge of our collaboration was that his dog was sick. The pit bull, he told me, had just undergone an unanticipated surgery and the vet bill was astronomical, so could I be a little more lenient on pricing, and would I accept installments? Jews and Arabs—is there so much difference between us really? I agreed, since our much-loved dog was still very much alive then and I knew all too well the cost of keeping her that way. A few days later I received a large brown package by courier, the contents of which were two massive dossiers of counterintelligence data. It was fitting that at the time my office was in a basement space in SoHo where only those with a key and an appetite for underground bunkers would ever set foot. No doubt the messenger thought I was someone far more interesting than I am. I sat at my desk and pored over every page until the sun passed behind the building next door, casting my office into darkness. With bare lightbulbs in fixtures that were mounted on the exposed brick wall, the scene had all the trappings of a suspense thriller. And I hadn't even gotten to the Crazy Wall yet. For weeks during and after working with this gentleman, every time I got a spam call or a weird email, paranoia told me it was the feds. I was on some kind of list, I thought. I had to be.

Amused by how surreal it all was, I decided to tell my family about it at our next family dinner, thinking they'd find it interesting. I didn't give any details, of course, just a high-level description of the engagement, but before I could even tell them about the dog, they were barking at me for agreeing to work with a Saudi. "How could you?!" my Scottish mother shrieked at me. "Would you work with Hitler if he called?" She's not a fan of Saudis, and this was before the crown prince ordered the barbaric murder of journalist Jamal Khashoggi, had him cut into pieces, and then smuggled the pieces out of an embassy. The dinner erupted into a shouting match about the Middle East while I slunk away to the kitchen, wondering whether I had made a miscalculation in not considering the ethics of the other party. I never even got to tell them about my hilarious wasabi joke.

I may not have sold you on my principle that humor has a place in almost any type of speech. It goes without saying that there are rare moments where gravity and seriousness must not be leavened with humor, but you're unlikely to find yourself making the kind of speech in which this is the case. I'm talking president in a pandemic—those kind of stakes. (If you do one day become a world leader, I hope this book played a tiny part in getting you there. Unless you're an autocrat, in which case I take zero responsibility.) Nevertheless, I hope you'll at least consider that the absence of humor should never owe to a lack of confidence on the speaker's part. It breaks my heart how often people pull the humor out of the drafts I send them, simply because of fear of failure.

I make it a point to press any client who removes jokes to ask why, so we can at least surface the concern and talk about it. I would say I manage to put the levity back in about 80 percent of the time. It's often just a question of me reading it out loud so they can hear what the line sounds like in the context of the paragraph. Humor—like the rest of the speech—is so reliant on the delivery. This is why I encourage everyone to participate in a delivery session, not just to smooth out any bumps but also to find the emotional texture, the shifts in energy, and the perfect execution of the punchlines. To me a speech is not a speech until it is taken off the page, and so my work is incomplete with those who don't spare the time to do this session. I still very much believe that, and I'll talk more about this later.

Our friend Winston Churchill's list of key elements missed the one component that, in my opinion, cannot be overstated. To me, humor is essential. Even in our most earnest or saddest moments, humans find comfort and connection with each other through humor. When we laugh together, in that moment the laughter is all that's happening—judgments and distracted thoughts, begone. Bringing an audience together into a collective experience is the ultimate goal of a speech, and no device does that better than a good joke. I still talk today about a corker I heard at my best friend's wedding. The groom was speaking about his recently deceased father and expressing regret that his father had never met the woman who was now his wife. Given how many brothers and sisters the groom had, how sudden and tragic his father's death had been, and how close the bride's and groom's families had become, the absence of a father figure on his side on the day was felt by all. And the groom himself was quite the prankster, so this thoughtful tribute was all the more poignant.

"My biggest regret is that my father never met Chiara," he said. "I know he would have loved her." Then there was a short beat. "He always was a boob man."

For this very English, booze-loving, country-living crowd, who care nothing for political correctness, the punchline was perfect. Chiara's ample bra size was undeniable; she's proudly joked about her breasts her whole life. Authentic and raunchy, the joke broke right through the moment of tragedy and transitioned the mood seamlessly back to celebration. Ten years later we're still chuckling about how much everyone laughed.

Being funny in a speech is not as hard as you might think. You don't have to be a naturally witty raconteur or a stand-up comedian to make your audience smile or laugh out loud. What comedians do is hard because they've made a promise to be hilarious and have thus set an expectation they must satisfy. When it comes to average speakers, it is certainly not taken for granted that they will be hysterically funny. Which means that you don't have to work to earn the audience's approval—they're delighted to even be able to smile. The bar is low.

Remember the celebrity emcee and former athlete, the one with the ultra-controlling publicist? Well, the second set of substantial remarks he made at the opening-night party were about the host city. His words would follow a slickly produced video featuring two well-known recording artists performing an original song to a backdrop of beautiful imagery of the people and the place. The takeaway would be its innovation, a city at the center of it all. It was a city my client had genuinely loved, where he'd lived very happily for years while playing for the team. So, obviously, I asked what he didn't like about it. He answered very definitively: the traffic. (A dead giveaway that he was originally a suburban or rural boy!)

"Great," I said, somewhat unsurprised, but happy to try to crack open this teensy-weensy nugget of personal content. "Tell me in as much detail as you can about your drive from the airport to the training field, what you see, what route you take, who you pass." The very specific details he provided, paired with my use of Google Maps to check for alternative routes and landmarks, made for a perfect personal tribute to the city, and his description of that very singular commute was a nice complement to the glossier and more generic portrayal of the city seen in the video. Most importantly, by reminiscing about the journey he was then able to make a reluctant admission that he even missed "the damn traffic lights, the only thing this innovative city needs to innovate a lot more." It was not a hilarious joke by any stretch of the imagination, but one of very few, and a nice callback to the innovation piece mentioned earlier.

There are many genres of comedy. Since I'm hilariously ill-equipped to speak about those, if you're in the market for a lesson on comedy, allow me to recommend a Judd Apatow MasterClass. I will say, though, that when it comes to comedic devices such as puns, innuendos, and double entendres, I don't find myself often drawn to these kinds of structures unless they're staring me in the face. Such was the case for another very good friend's father in yet another unforgettable wedding moment back in the UK. "I'll never forget meeting my new son-in-law for the first time," he said. "He stuck his hand out very enthusiastically and said, 'Hi, I'm Rich.' I thought, well that's a good start." It was so obvious, but it was perfect. Emily's father isn't a comedy writer, but the double entendre was right there in his lap. How could he *not* have made a joke about his son-in-law being Rich?

The jokes I write are what Apatow might call anecdotal. Some are roasty. Some are sarcastic. Some are dry, some are punchy. Some are merely moments of levity aimed at eliciting a smile rather than a fully charged belly laugh. But whatever form the humor takes, without exception it emerges from the very real material. If you took the joke out, you'd still have a complete speech. It might have less impact, but nevertheless, the content would not be compromised. This is what separates humor in speech from a stand-up set; a comparison that is laid bare in the acceptance speech Tina Fey gave when she received the Mark Twain Prize for American Humor in 2010—one of my favorites. Fey is a comedian, so the entire top half of her speech is a setup and punchline followed by a setup and punchline. I've highlighted the jokes to show how if you took them out you'd be left with very little.

> *Thank you very much. Thank you so much. Thank you all for dressing up.* **God. Listening to all of these speeches and performances for the last two hours, I cannot help but feel grateful that I put a bag of pretzels in my purse.**
>
> *I want to thank everyone involved with the Kennedy Center,* **or as it will soon be known, The Tea Party Bowling Alley and Rifle Range. It's gonna look good, we can get about nine lanes in here. I want to thank everyone at WETA, and PBS, not just for televising this event, but for showing** *The Benny Hill Show* **so much when I was a kid. I don't know how that qualified to be on PBS—we may never know.**
>
> **I promise to put this award in a place of honor to make sure that my daughter does not pretend that it is Barbie's older husband, who lost his body in an accident.**
>
> *I never dreamed that I would receive the Mark Twain*

Prize for American Humor. Mostly because my style is so typically Austrian.

I never thought I would even qualify for the Mark Twain Prize for American Humor. I mean, maybe the Nathaniel Hawthorne Prize for Judgmental Nature, or the Judy Blume Award for Awkward Puberty, or the Harper Lee Prize for Small Bodies of Work. But never this. And yet, I hope that like Mark Twain, a hundred years from now, people will see my work and think, "Wow, that is actually pretty racist."

Apparently I'm only the third woman to ever receive this award, and I'm so honored to be numbered with Lily Tomlin and Whoopi Goldberg, but I do hope that women are achieving at a rate these days that we can stop counting what number they are at things.

Yes, I was the first female head writer at Saturday Night Live, *and yes, I was only the second woman ever to be pregnant while on the show. And now tonight I am the third female recipient of this prize.* I would love to be the fourth woman to do something, but I just don't see myself married to Lorne.

I'm so grateful to my friends who came here tonight to perform. Some people came all the way from Los Angeles, and I know that you are all very busy people with families and it means so much to me to know that you care about show business more than you do about them.

I want to thank Alec Baldwin for not coming tonight. I already have a reputation as a liberal elite lunatic, I don't need that guy followin' me around. Johnny-Huffington-Post. *Actually I do want to thank Alec genuinely for staying in New York tonight, to continue to shoot at 30 Rock, so that I could be here, so thank you, Alec, I love you.*

I'm not gonna get emotional tonight, because I am a stone-cold bitch. *But I want to thank my family.* They say that funny people often come from a difficult childhood, or a troubled family, so to my family, I say, "They're giving me the Mark Twain Prize for American Humor, what did you animals do to me?" Yeah.

I know my mother and father are so proud of me tonight, so this is probably a good time to tell them, I'm putting you both in a home. We'll talk about it later.

I met my husband, Jeff, when we were both in Chicago and I had short hair with a perm on top and I would wear oversized denim shorts over-alls, and that is how I know our love is real.

At some point in the future, our daughter Alice will find a DVD of this broadcast, or I don't know, download it into the subdermal iPhone in her eyelids, I don't know how far in the future we're talking about. But I hope that it will make her laugh, and it will explain to her why her parents looked so tired all the time.

The one person without whom I really would not be here tonight, except of course for my mother, who is pretty sure she delivered me even though she had a lot of twilight sleep, *the other one person is Lorne Michaels.*

If you take away the highlighted jokes, what is left is nothing much beyond thank-yous to the hosts, her friends, and her family, which an award recipient is obliged to give anyway. The jokes in this case are there to entertain, since the substance itself is not insightful, educational, or inspiring in the least. In the second half of the speech, which begins with the story of her first meeting with Michaels, the relationship between the humor and the substance shifts. Here the jokes are there not to entertain but to elevate and add spice to a more profound message, which even without the punchlines still has a lot to say about Fey's journey into comedy and how she feels about being a comedian in this time and space.

> *In 1997 I flew from Chicago to New York to have a job interview for a writing position at* Saturday Night Live. *And I was hopeful because I'd heard the show was looking to diversify, which, by the way, only in comedy is an obedient white girl from the suburbs a diversity candidate. But, I remember, you know, I came for my job interview and the only decent clothes I had at the time, Lorne was right, was I had a pair of black pants and a sweater from Contempo Casuals. And I went to the security guard at the elevator at 30 Rockefeller Plaza, and I said "I'm here to see Lorne Michaels" and I couldn't believe the words that were coming out of my mouth: "I'm here to see Lorne Michaels."*
>
> *And I went up to the seventeenth floor and I had my meeting with Lorne, and the only thing anyone had told me about meeting with Lorne, having a job interview, they said, "Whatever you do, do not finish his sentences." A girl I knew in Chicago had done that and she felt like*

it had cost her the job, and so, whatever you do, don't finish his sentences. And I was there and really didn't want to blow it and Lorne said, "So, you're from ...," and it just was hanging there, "So, you're from ...," and I found I couldn't take any more, and I said, "Pennsylvania, I'm from Pennsylvania, suburb of Philadelphia," just as Lorne was finishing his thought and said, "Chicago," and I thought, That's it. I blew it. And I don't remember anything else about the meeting, because I just kept staring at him thinking, "This is the guy from the Beatles sketch! I can't believe that I'm in his office."

And you know, I could never have guessed that a couple years later I would be sitting in that office until two, three, four in the morning, thinking, "If this meeting doesn't end, I'm gonna kill this Canadian bastard."

The last time I was in Washington was in 2004 to take this Life magazine cover photo with John McCain. And Senator McCain gave my husband and me a tour of the Senate, and we all spent a lovely, busy afternoon together. And I have it on good authority that this picture of Senator McCain and myself has been hanging in his office, by his desk since 2004. And he has been looking at it every day since 2004, getting ideas. So I guess what I'm saying is, this whole thing might be my fault.

I would be a liar and an idiot if I didn't thank Sarah Palin for helping get me here tonight. My partial resemblance and her crazy voice are the two luckiest things that ever happened to me.

All kidding aside, I'm so proud to represent American humor. I'm proud to be American. I'm proud to make my home in the Not Real America. And I am most proud *that even during trying times, like an orange alert, or a bad economy, or a contentious election, that we as a nation retain our sense of humor. Anyway, I don't wanna go on and on, because I know we still have to talk about the other four nominees, so thank you and good night.*

No one has ever complained about a speech being too funny, but they certainly complain if it tries and fails. My hope is that this chapter will spare you from this fate. But there are other traps still lurking for the aspiring joke-writer. Humor in the context of a speech depends on who is its target and who is its consumer. You likely read the transcript of Tina Fey's speech and got every punchline because as a comedian (sketch, stand-up, or otherwise), she can make only broad assumptions about her audience's demographic, political leanings, and values. In a speech where an audience can be more sharply defined, the jokes can be more nuanced and specific to the exact people in the room. What might be funny to a group of engineers, for example, might be unintelligible to a room full of health and fitness experts. But within that audience, you have to walk a line between a cultural or familial reference and a private joke that alienates anyone who wasn't part of the team or wasn't there. I always say that if less than 50 percent of the audience will get the joke, don't bother. If there isn't a way of piecing together the joke that brings everyone in on it, then chances are it's the type of private joke that few people outside the group "in the know" will find funny anyway. Another red flag is if you find yourself qualifying the story or the joke with "it was so funny." That's a warning you haven't worked hard enough to make it funny for everyone.

I was surprised to find out that PBS in fact cut a section from its broadcast of the award ceremony. After Fey mentioned Palin, she went on:

> *Politics aside, the success of Sarah Palin and women like her is good for all women—except, of course, those who will end up paying for their own rape kit and stuff. But for everybody else, it's a win-win. Unless you're a gay woman who wants to marry your partner of twenty years. Whatever. But for most women, the success of conservative women is good for all of us. Unless you believe in evolution. You know—actually, I take it back. The whole thing's a disaster.*

Either Fey made a serious miscalculation about her audience or, more likely, she was speaking to a community that she felt would be able to see through their political bias and appreciate the humor. She didn't, however, factor in the broadcaster. The fact that those in the control room didn't feel as though that particular part of her remarks aligned enough with their nonpartisan programming highlights a complication to the concept of audience. When you're being filmed and aired on TV, is your audience the room or the world beyond it, and how much should that matter? (I wonder if Fey thought about that and intentionally included that section about Palin anyway.) I don't think there is a right answer; it's up to you to decide how expansive your appeal is and what is or isn't sacrificed as a result.

It can certainly make you unpopular if your humor comes at the expense of someone else. Fey obviously doesn't give a crap about Sarah Palin, but it's a mistake often committed by overly ambitious novice roasters at weddings and other celebratory events. Causing a person embarrassment with vulgar stories or exposés of their most disturbing secrets is awkward for everyone, can be unproductive for your own reputation, and in extreme cases can even incite vengeful retaliation. Just look what happened after Obama ripped into Trump at the White House Correspondents' Dinner in 2011! The exception to these guidelines of mild civility—because remember, there are no fixed rules in speechmaking—is the Friars Club roasts, because the entire point of these roasts is to be as mean as possible to the guest of honor by making up as much shit about them as possible. At the roast of Rob Lowe in 2016, Pete Davidson took down fellow guest Ann Coulter, with this joke: "You know, last year we had Martha Stewart, who sells sheets, and now we have Ann Coulter, who cuts eyeholes in them." Ouch. I hope she doesn't run for president. . . .

Speaking of Obama's White House Correspondents' Dinner speeches, in his eighth and final year in office, the president's opening gambit showed a brilliant example of how to create jokes from your material by simply making connections like those we talked about in the Crazy Wall chapter.

"If this material works well," he said, "I'm going to use it at Goldman Sachs next year." Then he paused. "Earn me some serious Tubmans." You can see so clearly how in this 2016 speech he threaded the needle between Hillary's controversial speaking fees and the proposed redesign of the $20 bill (which Trump's treasury secretary, Steve Mnuchin, then canceled—and Biden later reinstated). If you've made some version of the Crazy Wall, those connections are easier to spot and the jokes suddenly take shape where you least expected them.

The Room for Laughter

All the jokes I write come directly from things I spot in the material—the incongruities, contradictions, and coincidences. The exercise is exactly the same as it is when identifying connections and relationships for larger framework pieces, such as the sofa in Adrianne's speech.

In another example, while working with a very outspoken woman on her inaugural speech as president of a Jewish congregation, I saw in her answers to my questions that she'd collaborated closely with the CEO on a full renovation of the synagogue and that they'd argued about the beautiful exposed brick she'd wanted and the necessary soundproofing of the sanctuary. She'd already opened the speech by confessing that she might not be the most observant Jew in the land but that she would be the loudest and most vocal in doing what was best for the community. The joke was right there in plain sight:

> *One of my favorite things we've recently done is, of course, the renovation. What a joy it was to watch Ira work his magic. I bet he wished he could have put up a few extra soundproof panels when I was nagging him about the exposed brick.*

I've been reading people's stories, ideas, and miscellaneous tidbits for so long that one of the first things I notice as I gather the material is how the disparate pieces create the right tension for humor. I scribble notes as soon as a joke pops into my head so I can return to it later. I never know where a joke might fit into the speech or whether it will even make it in, but I never skip an opportunity. Once you start being able to recognize these contradictions and coincidences in your material, creating jokes from them requires only a dash of imagination and courage—imagination, to be able to conjure up a picture of the most extreme or ludicrous outcome between two sets of circumstances you've identified, and courage, to commit to the joke without apology or extra words that circumvent rather than drive directly to the joke.

Take George W. Bush's eulogy for his father. Early in his sincere and witty tribute Bush spoke about George senior's vigor in his old age:

> *At age ninety, George H. W. Bush parachuted out of an aircraft and landed on the grounds of St. Anne's by the Sea in Kennebunkport, Maine, the church where his mom was married and where he worshipped often. Mother liked to say he chose the location just in case the chute didn't open.*

It was a lovely moment in an otherwise somber setting. Regardless of whether Barbara Bush really did say that, the joke was crafted by imagining the very worst scenario in which the forty-first president parachuted to his death.

I wrote a similar line in a speech for Celine, an event planner with whom I've collaborated a number of times. She'd been unwell due to exhaustion, but she was fond of promoting an image of herself as the irrepressible doyenne of party planning. Reflecting on her health, and armed with everything I knew about her expertise in lighting, catering, and the works, I wrote:

> *My medical bills alone show how hard the team and I have been working. This past year nearly killed me. I quite literally ran a movie premiere after-party while hooked up to an IV after I got an infection and had surgery. I didn't go to the*

event itself, obviously—a drip doesn't blend in so well no matter how dimly you light the bar.

I opened my mind to the absurd—what it would have looked like to go to the event with a IV trolley in tow—and hey presto, the lighting became a central piece to the joke. I could even have taken it a step further and pretended she did go. An alternative line could have been: *I got an infection and had surgery and I think I was still hooked up the IV when I ran an after-party event the following week. Thank God the venue had dimmers.*

I said you need courage, and some speakers aren't comfortable with artistic license. My client in this case was nervous her audience might believe she went to the event while carting around an intravenous drip (events people—not so bright, apparently), so we tempered it ever so slightly without killing the joke completely. But stretching the truth for a joke is completely acceptable—there's a gulf between using artistic license for humor and outright lying. In Celine's case, lying would have been to say: *I turned up to run a party and had an IV in tow all night—thank God for the dimmers.* You can see the difference. The wording in the first makes the truth ambiguous. In the second the truth is entirely changed.

One of the most satisfying jokes I've ever written was for a best man in California. We'll call him Aziz. He had given me extremely funny material to work with already just on account of how eccentric and outrageous his friend Taylor was, so I was off to a flying start. Earlier in the speech we'd used college stories about the groom to address his character. One anecdote told of his compulsion for hosting huge parties on campus complete with disco balls and smoke machines. He would spend untold sums of money on creating the right vibe—a beer keg and Solo cups alone were far too gauche. But the real gift came when Aziz showed me an article from the *New York Times* reporting a gas pipe explosion right by Taylor's apartment, specifically a quote made by Taylor to a reporter that day.

This is how we tied it all together in the speech about three-quarters of the way through:

> *Taylor was actually in the* New York Times, *though— unlike* The Lord of the Rings, *which he never made it into. The headline of the article was:* "Displaced by Pipe Blast Contamination, Residents Seek Answers." *According-ing to the reporter, Taylor was anxious about the possible effects of asbestos exposure, and as he carried a bag of the clothes he had been wearing the day of the explosion to drop off at the laundry, he was quoted as saying:* "It's a little nerve-racking when you see people in hazmat suits."
>
> *I found this surprising. He was so worried about as-bestos when he was never once concerned about what was in that smoke machine.*

I knew the unexpected reference to the smoke machine from much earlier in the speech would draw laughter. The callback is a highly effective comedy device, and one I use repeatedly. The original reference to the thing doesn't have to have been funny. It could just be part of the exposition, as in the case of Deja Foxx—a very charismatic activist and Gen Z POTUS-in-the-making—with whom I worked in 2018.

Deja was speaking to a roomful of politically engaged advocates and organizers, and she wanted to tell them a bit of her story they didn't know and give them a sense of where she was coming from. She'd shot to fame on Instagram for contesting Senator Jeff Flake on pro-choice issues at a town hall and had subsequently become the darling of Planned Parenthood supporters and clued-in feminists alike. Think AOC in a crop top and a lot of nail art. At the top of the speech she told the starry-eyed crowd about growing up in Arizona and working at a gas station where the most infuriating part of her job behind the counter was figuring out how to properly dispense the soft-serve ice cream. "For six months I really struggled with that winding motion. They'd come out lopsided every time," she confessed in the setup. But the real kicker came at the end. By now she'd moved on to the kind of constituents she represented, the type of faces she wanted to see in Congress, and the kind of representative America could expect if she ever made it there.

> *The media outlets are going to have a hard time describing me when I get to Congress.*
> *So I've made a list of words they can choose from: smart, resilient, passionate, unapologetic, and super fucking awesome with a soft-serve machine. Hard to label and impossible to replace. Just like the people I represent.*

The crowd went wild. The callback combined with the expletive came out the blue and left the room intoxicated by its youthful energy. I hope when she becomes president she calls me. I'll be just old enough to be pissed off about the next young speechwriter telling me I'm doing it all wrong.

Of course, the delivery Deja gave it was everything in this context. She pierced the air with the index fingers of both hands, and the blood-red-painted talons protruding from them infused the atmosphere with her street-smart swagger.

Delivery plays a key role in comedy, but just as the craft of these jokes finds roots in the material itself, the delivery has everything to do with the personality of the speaker. If you've managed to write a good joke, then you'll know exactly how to deliver it. There isn't a right or wrong way, especially when you're talking about anecdotal comedy, where the humor is less dependent on a laugh line than it is on the circumstance you've fabricated or highlighted. Playing the truth of the moment will be your most effective weapon. Are you surprised? Are you delighted? Are you disapproving? Do you deliver with conviction because you know the thing to be true, as with Deja and her soft-serve? Or are you still puzzled, as Aziz was with Taylor's concern about asbestos? Or perhaps innocence is the sentiment you're going for, like my Saudi friend.

He never did use the wasabi joke, but in the end, though the play on words may have failed, you might say farce prevailed. Once I'd completed my work I sent my final invoice, which was really a reminder for remittance of the first invoice and a balance statement for the total. Two weeks later I received my second brown envelope from him. This time it wasn't stuffed with Saudi propaganda; it was filled neatly with wads of cash, to the tune of a few thousand dollars. To borrow from *Sex and the City*'s heroine and TV's other famous Carrie—I couldn't help but wonder, did he pay the vet bill this way too?

12

Stand and Deliver

Practicing Alone for Your Audience

I've said from the very beginning that a speech isn't a speech until it comes off the page. Yet so many people with whom I've worked over the years have overlooked my offer of a delivery session as a bonus—if time permits. By the time we've completed the draft and have agreed on its final revision, I can only assume that, newly emboldened by the content and substance of their remarks, they feel ready for their audience. This is indeed satisfying, I confess. But delivery is a fundamental aspect of the preparation, and no matter how seasoned you are, there is always room for growth—especially when you're handling brand-new material.

I was pleased that Dominic brought this up before even I did. A superstar entrepreneur fresh out of an Ivy League business school, Dominic was the founder of an industry-disrupting business whose pitch-perfect branding had seduced millions of millennial American consumers. He had told his story a million times in interviews, on panels, and in keynotes—but despite his relative fame, the whirlwind of media attention, and the cadence of his press calendar, he found he still struggled to speak in public in a confident and convincing manner. Dominic was looking for a departure from his boilerplate talking points, and his goal with our collaboration was to offer not only a fresh message to the students at his alma mater but a polished delivery of which he could be proud. We worked on the script, edited and finalized it, and then he vanished. I sent a couple of emails to remind him that we still had to work on the delivery, but not a single missive was returned. No emails, no calls. I even had to chase him for payment. I felt like an abandoned wife demanding alimony.

It was unfortunate indeed. But the most disconcerting moment of all was that a month or so later I had a poke around the internet, and lo and behold found a video of his address on YouTube. I suspected that he must have been dissatisfied with the outcome of our work together, and so I braced myself before I pressed play, expecting a complete departure from our message—a round trip, if you will, back to his hackneyed media script. I don't know what was most astonishing: the fact that he had not changed a word or beat of the speech we wrote, or the way he mumbled and spluttered his way through it. In the end he too had underestimated the importance of the delivery.

I'm already thinking about delivery way before the client is, in a way that even Dominic wasn't. As I compose the script I'm not only thinking about the clarity and impact of the language, I'm thinking about the phrasing, pacing, rhythm, and emphasis. As the drafting process continues into the revision stage and finally to a delivery session, the formatting of the text on the page starts to evolve with the needs of the client to satisfy these key elements and support them as the words come alive. Until this point the audience has been a north star for so many choices made on this journey, but when it comes to shepherding a client through the delivery, the techniques I employ are now almost exclusively informed by the speaker—by their ability to connect to the narrative we have crafted and by the personality they bring to the text.

I can't tell you how often a client has misunderstood something I wrote or not fully grasped the meaning until I gave them a reading of it myself. Just as a great line on the page can be butchered by an ineffectual delivery, the transcript of a speech can obscure its full effect. A joke might not seem as funny; a powerful line might not convey its force.

For an example of the latter, take this sweet little jab of Biden's during the 2020 presidential debates: "Trump sees the climate as a joke. I see jobs." On paper? Nothing special. But with derision in his voice in the first half of the line, a quick beat and then a very earnest turn imbued with optimism, he delivered the second to great effect. Which is saying something for President Biden, whom I find lacking in the oratory department.

The incongruity between the written phrase and its impact can sometimes be put down to the deft skill of the orator, but often—at least, if you're reading something I've written—it may well be due to the unorthodox punctuation and formatting. Generally speaking, the drafts I compose use few punctuation marks beyond the dash and the "full stop," as I grew up calling it. (To British women the word "period" is used only to describe an altogether different -ation than the punctu- variety, and it's been very challenging to adapt.) Just as in musical composition slurs and accents define the phrasing, when I write I'm thinking of how it plays to the ear. I use dashes to show where one thought can be broken up into phrases to allow for breath and asides, as in the following example:

> *You know, today is actually my last official appearance on behalf of [name of company]. I co-founded it twenty-two years ago and—I might be the first and only person to ever say this at the Chamber of Commerce—I feel a little bit emotional.*

When I do use a period (cringe!) in a place that might feel forced or premature in the thought, it is precisely because I wish to make a larger point or separate two smaller thoughts for emphasis. My second-grade grammar teacher would, I'm sure, faint on discovering how often I follow it with a capitalized conjunction like "but" or "and." But I do so knowing that what comes next needs its own space. As that just did. I also often use a line break for further emphasis. This is the continuation of the excerpt above:

> *I knew this day would come of course—I've been preparing for it for a while.*
>
> *You see these fashionable sneakers and my casually unbuttoned shirt? All very well thought out to align with my personal transformation. In the past, my typical uniform for this type of event would have been a blue suit, white shirt, and dark blue tie.*
>
> *But that style no longer suits my strategy.*
>
> *On August 31, my last day as CEO, I did what most C-suite executives do to celebrate their retirement.*
>
> *I went to Burning Man.*
>
> *For those of you who don't know what that is, let's*

just say there are a lot of people, a lot of art, a lot of crazy costumes, and it's all in the middle of the desert. And it was there—at Burning Man—under an immense temporary sanctuary—built from thirty huge pieces of wood converging as a spiral toward the sky— with a 3D-printed Buddhist symbol of self-unity in the center—it was there that I sat alone and allowed myself to disconnect spiritually and emotionally from the company I had created.

It was a powerful moment.

You should have seen my outfit for that.

So why am I telling you all this? Surely not just for the opportunity to regale you with stories of my recent fashion evolution.

No.

Not really.

It's because in that moment of reflection, I was able to think about the last twenty-two years. What I'd achieved. How I'd changed. What I might have done differently. And how I was going to use what I'd learned to move forward.

During the delivery practice with this client, as with any other, I tinkered even more with punctuation and formatting to clarify where the emotional shifts, energy changes, stillnesses, and throwaways were. The fun thing about the document you craft is that it's entirely yours and yours alone—no one is going to see the text, so you have permission to use whatever punctuation helps you pace yourself or gear up for a big punchline. As you read it through aloud and make final tweaks to any of the substance that doesn't make logical sense, you can add in all the dashes and periods, slashes, boldface, and line breaks you want. As long as you know what they all mean.

Over the years I've used many different tactics to indicate changes in emphasis, tone, energy, and subject. Charlie's forty-minute speech, for instance, was color-coded to indicate where each new "chapter" started.

I have often found that bolding a word in the sentence helps with emphasis, especially in cases where hitting a different word can change the sentiment behind the line. For example:

> *Justice Ginsburg spent her career trying to break down and rebuild the scaffolding of our society so that a woman didn't have to shatter a glass ceiling to compete with a man.*

Without any specific direction, my client gave emphasis to "glass ceiling," which is understandable. So I bolded the word "have."

> *Justice Ginsburg spent her career trying to break down and rebuild the scaffolding of our society so that a woman didn't* **have** *to shatter a glass ceiling to compete with a man.*

The image of the glass ceiling is a well-worn metaphor, so we weren't trying to point it out so much as say that RBG was fighting for women long before we universally started to think of the gender imbalance in such terms—before the ceiling became crystallized, so to speak. When the stress falls on the word "have," it acknowledges that the ceiling already exists.

The difference is subtle and certainly not game-changing alone, but ten or so missed opportunities to strengthen a point add up. A good example of the impact of this escalation was a female executive who kept putting the emphasis on the pronoun "I" in every sentence. So instead of articulating that she'd **missed** seeing her friends and colleagues in person but that she was **optimistic** about the future, she would say that **she'd** missed her friends and colleagues but **she** was optimistic, as if somehow suggesting no one else had or was. The over-enunciation of the "I" throughout made her sound unintentionally self-absorbed, which she certainly wasn't. Bolding the words that conveyed the emotion she wanted to share neither tripped her up nor distracted her in mid-delivery.

Remember those nice silent transitions where you can change the subject without having to say you're changing the subject? If I know we need that much space to give rise to a completely new idea, then I begin a new paragraph and insert the instruction "breathe" in brackets between the two. Why "breathe" instead of, say, "pause"? Because taking a moment to inhale organically reinvigorates and in this case reminds the speaker that an injection of fresh energy is required to begin the next thought. As Jenna Bush Hager did when discussing her grandfather's legacy, you need to signal to the audience with your voice. If I were to direct the speaker to pause, they might well just hold on to the breath and then continue on with whatever dregs of spirit they had left over. Worse, they might take this as a cue to stop for too long a period. And we've all sat through a speech and willed the speaker to just get the hell on with it. There is a fine balance to be mastered between clear enunciation and good pacing, on the one hand, and a stilted, lackluster performance, on the other. Sometimes I use italics to indicate where I want the client to drive right through the line rather than belabor the delivery. Often the intention is to deliver the thought as if it just occurred to the speaker in that moment, unscripted and improvised. It's what I call "a throwaway." Or sometimes it's just to make sure that the audience hears a meaty point in its entirety. The danger with an overly punctuated and extended execution is that the point gets lost or the audience becomes fatigued.

Whatever formatting helps you, it's helpful to drop these hints throughout the text to keep your pacing fluid, fully charged, and engaging. But it must be stated that clever formatting can only go so far. A show-off is a show-off and an introvert is an introvert. No amount of hyphens is going to change that. The good news is that improving delivery doesn't require a personality transplant. And it would be futile to try to turn a nervous, bookish nonprofit co-founder into a gung-ho motivational speaker like Mel Robbins or Tony Robbins (the two are unrelated, but wouldn't that be cute?). On the contrary, the audience wants to get to know the speaker, so pretending to be someone you're not isn't the answer.

My only goal is to turn you into your most confident, most articulate, and most charming self for a few minutes. If you've been through the exhaustive and exhilarating process of writing a speech, you'll already likely be operating on a higher level than you're used to. Your delivery should bring your remarks to life, not crush them under the weight of some phony alter ego.

Celine—of the IV drip dilemma—didn't need to hide behind an alternative. On the contrary, with a personality almost as large as her many-times-dyed bouffant hairdo, Celine dripped with diamonds as if she'd stepped out of an episode of the 1980s show *Dynasty* (look it up if you're too young) and sounded as if the show had been shot on location at Zabar's (ditto). Imagine Krystle Carrington meets Dolly Parton meets Mrs. Maisel. If you were looking for decadence and pink up-lighting, Celine was your gal. If you wanted to hear captivating stories, she was the most sublime raconteur one on one. Un-believably, though, to this industry icon and mentor to many, the idea of addressing a big crowd was intimidating. Her de-livery when we started working together was at best reticent.

Somehow I had to trick her into thinking she was in social mode instead of speech mode. It helped that while we were working on the speech her miniature poodle ran around close by with its gemstone collar tinkling, reminding Celine who was in charge. Occasionally she'd give the dog a ticking off the way people who let their dogs kiss them on the mouth do— delighted for the excuse to have a human-style interaction with their favorite furry friend. "Diamonds, go and harass May, Mommy is busy." (May was the housekeeper.) "Ma-a-a-y? Can you take Lady Di for a walk and bring me some lemonade on your way out?" Cue the silent arrival of two highball glasses filled with a freshly squeezed lemon beverage served with care on a silver tray to protect the lace and polyester tablecloth.

To be fair, Celine, for all her pomp and costume jewelry, was an extremely warm and kind matriarchal figure, and sincere with her affection once you were in the fold. After the first speech we wrote together she was so ecstatic with the results she wrote me a thank-you card, which she sent with a beautiful gift for our recently born first child. I still have the Bergdorf's gift receipt for the silk puffball dress she bought—no child of mine ever leaves the house in anything fancier than dirtied-up leggings for the playground, and I'm sure as hell not spending $200 on them!

Celine's problem wasn't that she was nervous about the spotlight. It was simply that being such a gifted storyteller, she'd never really had to script her stories before now. This was the first time that she needed the structure and objectives of a formal speech and she struggled to bring the printed words to life with the same expressive manner as when speaking in conversation. She stumbled and paused and misread the text and then got flustered, and it seemed clear that I needed to make the experience more empowering.

I knew from the hours of interviews that Celine and her team arrived at their events on the day each carrying a black binder with the run of show and all the info they would need to pull it off smoothly—emergency numbers, timings, layout diagrams, and so on. It occurred to me that this might be a prop that would reestablish Celine's sense of self. When we met for our second delivery session, I printed the speech in an enlarged font to make it easy for her to read, making sure that the new page breaks coincided with the end of a sentence each time so she wasn't flipping to another page mid-thought. Then I laminated the resulting forty or so pages—because I knew she loved lamination—and put them in a black binder. As we sat at her dining table, once again with May and Diamonds nearby, Celine gradually began to loosen up as she read. And by the time we got the speech on its feet, the effervescent Celine we all knew was back.

The first read-through in a delivery session with a client is a very casual, seated affair. The objective is to lock in the text once and for all so the speaker walks away knowing exactly what they need to do when they step up to the microphone. I can't stop speakers fiddling with their drafts after we meet for the last time, but my hope is that this is the script they take up to the podium unaltered.

This reading is not just to listen for stumbles or trip-ups. It's to notice whether at any point I get bored or distracted. By this stage I have read the damn thing out loud to myself more times than is natural, so my bored-o-meter is set pretty low. But when it comes to practicing one's own delivery, the ears must be sharpened in anticipation. Recognizing you are boring yourself requires honesty and humility. If even for a second you get the feeling you're phoning it in or there's filler that lags in energy or doesn't move the narrative on enough, take a pause and ask yourself whether it's extraneous or repetitive or too verbose. Can you cut it? Streamline it? Move it somewhere where it may make more sense? Add humor, perhaps? Don't ignore that feeling. If you lost interest, the audience most certainly will.

There's a charming concept called "killing your darlings." It's named this way to remind writers of their hubris when it comes to cutting their words. You may think this is the best story ever or the funniest part of the speech, but if it doesn't belong, it doesn't matter how much you love it, you've got to kill it. I am a bona fide child murderer at this point.

Once we've made the final tweaks and adjustments to the content, I ask the client to stand in some imitation of how they expect to present themselves on the day. Just as the writing is imbued with dynamism when taken off the page, it goes further when taken into the body. I promise I won't get too thespian, but physicality cannot be neglected here. The politician's shaken fist is physicality; pacing back and forth is physicality, for better or worse. When Churchill slammed his chest with the delivery of the line "While there is breath in our bodies" during an address to the US Congress in 1943, the impact rang throughout the great hall. That was physicality.

At this stage my feedback is simple and easy to digest for even the most amateurish: keep the feet still, hip width apart. Loosen the body from the waist up so you can turn from side to side to reach both edges of the room and create connection with audience members there and in between. Hold your script or notecards out in front of you, and when you start to speak, identify the farthest point in the room you're in and send the words there. That's not too much, is it? It's vital to find out ahead of time whether you'll be expected to hold something—a microphone, a statuette—and whether you'll have a podium or a teleprompter. The aim of the session is to reproduce as closely as possible the situation as it will be, so that there are no surprises on the day. If you're tempted to beat your chest in the practice round and then the day of the event you find you're holding a mic, a script, and a delicate champagne flute, your speech will certainly be the talk of the town for the fact that you spilled your drink over the mother of the bride.

The most common habit I see is that even if a speaker is able to keep their feet still, they cannot help but sway and swing their bodies back and forth, shifting weight from one leg to the other, like a dovening rabbi or a jack-in-the-box at the end of its spring. This kind of incessant motion is distracting for the viewer and a waste of energy that should be otherwise channeled and projected outward toward the audience. Think of that moment in a sci-fi or fantasy movie when the hero or villain opens their mouth and shoots out a stream of life force. You know the scene. Sometimes there are wails and shrieks; we don't necessarily need those. But it always originates from deep within the core and explodes out with power, filling the sky. So that's what I'm trying to get the speaker to match or at least mimic. Because imagine that moment in the movie, and manipulate the image so the person is shifting from left to right. And now envision they have one arm crossed over their chest protectively clutching the other arm, which hangs limply at their side holding a script. Not exactly a show of strength.

With some semblance of stage presence established, the first standing read-through tells me everything I need to know about how the speaker is going to bring their own personality to the text. While they're getting acquainted with their physical being in this new context, my attention turns to their natural speaking volume, rhythms, and cadence. As with Celine, it's not always what it looks like on the label. An introvert can display an excellent instinct when it comes to inflection and can deliver a punchline like a stand-up pro. But if the audience can't hear it because the speaker is afraid to project, that's a problem. Over the years I've developed a set of proprietary exercises that get to the heart of the most common deficiencies, all of which can be improved upon for the sake of the five to forty minutes their speech will last, but none of which significantly change the personality of the speaker. Exercises range from the absurd (pretending to read your speech to a room of five-year-olds) to the more absurd (you're hiding from cannibalistic zombies with unnaturally good hearing, and your speech is the only thing that will help you escape if you can share it with the person hiding with you). They help solve the following tendencies:

Monotone range
Lack of energy
Shyness
Over-performance
Earnestness
Speed (speaking too fast or too slowly)

Dario was painfully shy. When he knocked on the door of The Oratory Laboratory's HQ for his Creative Kickoff meeting in our very first year of operation, we couldn't believe that this diminutive boy was about to take over the family business. His father, Dario explained, had been a well-known diamond cutter in New York, and his unexpected passing had left his eldest son in charge, years before he'd been expecting to take the helm. The immediate challenge Dario was facing was how to eulogize his father before the entire senior body of the South African Diamond Corporation and his extensive Italian American family at St. Patrick's Cathedral in New York City. He wanted to pay tribute to his role model and beloved father, but he also needed to reassure his father's partners and clients that he was a worthy successor.

His speech spoke of his father's passion for beauty and the values he'd taught his son that so elegantly translated into the way he approached the craft and the business. Given the wonderful stories Dario shared and the lessons learned from his father, the speech practically wrote itself. But when it came time to take the speech off the page, I knew that to fill a space like St. Patrick's, Dario would need a lot of support. I wasn't looking to turn him into an extrovert; rather, I hoped to infuse his less visible attributes, like loyalty and honesty, with volume and vigor in the five to ten minutes of his speech.

Some people who talk too fast are incapable of talking too slowly. Likewise, someone who lacks volume and, dare I say, charisma is unlikely to ever suffer from being too boisterous or performative. With someone like Dario, to get the projection and energy to fill the cathedral I used the "Gladiator" technique, which I rebranded "The Daenerys Targaryen Effect" after *Game of Thrones*. Her army and dragons could kick Russell Crowe's butt. The exercise is to imagine you're standing in front of your troops psyching them up before battle, reminding them why they fight for you. You are talking to hundreds of thousands and they are spread far, so yes, you have to shout. With Dario, we had chosen to start with a quiet anecdote. His first words, "I remember once being in South Africa with my father," could have sounded like an intimate recollection revealed for the first time, but thanks to some delivery work it quickly came to sound more like a bold, declarative story opener.

Back when we were launching The Oratory Laboratory, Nathan and I used to joke that beyond words and formatting, a good suit or the right shade of lipstick would do wonders for a speaker's self-confidence in the delivery. It's not such a joke, of course, but the suit Dario brought to show us was the icing on the cake. He had stepped into the role in every way.

Dario never would have gone over the top; his innate character wouldn't have let him. But for those who tap into their bravery through such an exercise, you can always tone it down. The important thing is to allow yourself the freedom to experiment in the first place so you get to a place where you feel that vitality and effort in the moment. To be able to improve one's own delivery summons a great deal of courage and also humility. You have to identify whether your challenge is speed, energy, monotony, or any of the other obstacles, and accept that it may be more than one. It might seem like the obvious thing to do in this case would be to ask the opinion of someone who knows you, like a friend or a family member, but quite honestly I don't trust any of them to be objective. In my experience humans are driven by an innate desire to prove they are the smartest one in the room, and if you ask someone you know to listen to your speech and give feedback on the delivery using the rubric above, you'll only invite commentary as to what could be better in the content and everything you've done wrong. This may just be my family, of course, but I can recall being in the middle of a live delivery session at the home of a client when his wife blew in from a shopping trip and announced she'd changed part of his speech that she thought could be "better." After she blew back out, I tactfully told him that she had cocked it up completely. Thankfully, he agreed. The next time he hired me to help with a speech, I was relieved by his suggestion to meet at his office.

Practicing your speech need not take up hours of your time. I suggest clients run through it once a day in the week leading up to the event. The danger of overdoing it is that it can begin to feel over-rehearsed and performative, or that as you become more familiar with the material you become more desensitized to it. Worse still is that it brings out a sense of bravado. You begin to wonder, *What if I just riff a little here and improvise there?* Don't.

If you've done the work—you've asked the questions, you've plumbed the depths of your own knowledge and explored far beyond for your material, and you've harnessed your most creative instincts in putting the pieces together—you don't need your mother or husband to tell you all the things they'd have done differently. Nor do you need an event host to make your speech safe or more sanguine. But you can drastically improve the delivery just as you composed the piece, by using your own judgment. Don't be afraid to turn the dial up to maximum; you can always turn it down again. And keep in mind that you don't need to be anyone you're not either. If you don't feel super-confident, don't fake it. Own it and do your best. That's what the audience wants. Remember, until you need to call in the fire department, they're on your side.

A Final Word

*I've been reading through the material you sent
me—what a fascinating career. I'm excited to learn
more and in doing so develop a compelling piece
for the Piedmont students.*

*That said, I think I'd like to get on another call
before I send you questions. I'd love to hear about
your childhood in Savannah, your family, and
the challenges and highlights you experienced long
before you went to Wharton.*

I sent this email to Patricia very early on in our now long-standing relationship. Lauded as one of the most powerful women on Wall Street, a majority stakeholder of the largest minority-owned financial firm in the country, and an inspiration to leaders everywhere, Patricia receives accolades, awards, and invitations to keynotes more often than I receive robocalls from China. (It occurred to me toward the end of the Covid-19 pandemic that perhaps all this time these calls were trying to communicate an urgent message: "There's a really evil virus coming! It's airborne! You have to wear masks! But you don't need to disinfect your groceries!" And there we were, hanging up on them and making Anthony Fauci do all the work.)

A Final Word

Right from the start Patricia would give me only limited access to her life story. No matter how much I pushed, I never felt I had more than the cursory details of what she did, when, and who was involved. What I wanted to know was, how? How did she overcome the obstacles? How did she feel knowing she had to fight harder than her peers? I wasn't privy to the anguish, frustration, joy, relief, and triumph. I could write a sweet professional bio, but I couldn't have written an in-depth biography. She would always say she didn't want to bring her personal life into it, or she'd just ignore my cautious provocations.

Faced with gaping holes in the narrative, I tried to fill them in as best I could to craft remarks for commencements, galas, ribbon cuttings, conventions, and conference guest speaker spots, and in doing so tackled every theme you could imagine, given her career trajectory: from leadership to mentorship, from career growth to client relationships. We touched on her experience as a woman in engineering, but even then, it felt very safe, maybe even detached, and tethered to a resume-based narrative. I recall in one instance we had a slightly tense exchange over an impending award acceptance speech. Patricia was adamant she didn't want to allude in any way to her life in the South, and I believed that two light jokes alluding to her early proficiency in reading and obvious intelligence would give an otherwise dry script some humanity. In anticipation of a speech for a major infrastructure firm's Black employee network during Black History Month one year, I looked forward to perhaps prying open this well-guarded vault of personal experiences. But again the best I got was a slightly unimaginative acknowledgment of the American legacy of slavery and the work still to do. I couldn't help but feel she was intentionally avoiding getting too close to the material.

And so it went for years. We pulled different pieces from her career trajectory and cast them in new narratives with fresh angles depending on the audience and the goals for the speech. I couldn't understand why Patricia kept me at arm's length, and I blamed myself for not being able to penetrate a layer deeper in understanding the inner, emotional life of this impressive woman. If I could do it with every other client, why not Patricia? She was a Black woman who had risen up the ranks of the whitest, most male-dominated industries—there had to be so much she wasn't telling me.

And then, finally, the tables turned. The treasury department of the world's biggest tech company invited her to speak in the summer of 2020. The Covid-19 pandemic was raging and disproportionately killing people of color, the ground was still vibrating with the marching feet of the Black Lives Matter protesters—America had arrived at a long-overdue reckoning. In this deeply unstable cultural moment, this company, which was grappling with racism as so many Fortune 500 companies were doing, asked Patricia to address the finance team on the subject of diversity and inclusion. She would be expected, the host informed her, to provide action-based goals tied to her own unique personal story.

I'm not a big fan of this particular company—I intensely dislike the impact it has had on the environment and on small businesses. But I'm very grateful for the impact it had on Patricia. When I say the floodgates opened, it's not an exaggeration. It was the first time she had ever been asked how she'd attained the level of success she had as a Black woman. I had always assumed this to be the most crucial and most interesting aspect of her story, and yet, because no one had ever explicitly made the offer, all these years she'd deferred to a safer narrative for fear of making her audience uncomfortable, as she now confessed to me. Her response was a revelation, as much for me as it was for Patricia. I suddenly had a much clearer and more illuminating picture of her life—of how she overcame the obstacles of a childhood in the Jim Crow South, how the lessons her parents had passed on had shaped her early thinking, and how she'd bent the rules in her determination not to be crushed by them. I heard about not just the successes but also the challenges preceding them. About being a Black female engineer trying to get a job on white-male-dominated Wall Street. Being pregnant and trying to hide it, but not being able to hide her skin color. I heard her speak, for the first time with emotional honesty, about the atrocities of the summer of 2020. She was more passionate and unrestrained than I had ever seen her. These were parts of her story she'd felt unable to share in the past, but they were also the parts that made her who she was.

The day before the event Patricia sent me an email, and even in this her new openness was recognizable. She was ecstatic to finally be presenting a truer version of her professional ascent and her vision for a more equitable world of business. I had never heard her say she "loved" anything, let alone describe something as perfection. People at Patricia's level don't see perfection; they see room for improvement. I've also never seen so many exclamation points. Knowing her as I did, I could see that this experience had been a catharsis.

Speaking in public—sharing something you know and care about—has exactly this effect. It can change the way people think and the way they behave. It can also be life-changing for you, the speaker. The impact of expressing yourself about something important in a way that captures the attention and imagination of an audience in the room can carry over into your day-to-day life and change the way you go about the world.

Like any endeavor with such high reward, nothing about it is easy or convenient. It requires rigor, humility, courage, imagination, and integrity. That's a lot to ask of anyone in one go, and it doesn't guarantee much. After you've interrogated your ideas, questioned your methods, and edited your words, you still won't know that you've succeeded. But you'll know you've at least done your very best.

There, I've said enough—it's your turn to speak.

Acknowledgments

My most humble thanks are to the many speakers who over the years have trusted me with their material and who have welcomed me into their lives to tangle with their most precious thoughts and ideas. Their triumphs, their tragedies, their challenges, and the things they hold most dear have been an endless source of inspiration and learning. There is no doubt that I am smarter and better at what I do for having heard their stories and "met" their audiences. I am grateful every day for the work and for the relationships it has forged.

For about three years before I even started working on the proposal for this book, I had an afternoon blocked out in purple on my calendar every week that declared "Book writing—Nonnegotiable!" And every week I very easily negotiated my way out of it. I had no idea how to write a book at that point, I only knew that there should be one. No amount of research or imagination can help put into words the immensity of my gratitude to Stephen Hanselman and Julia

Acknowledgments

Serebrinsky for believing this too and for their wisdom and guidance as I faced the challenge. I simply could never have done it without them, no matter what a motivational speaker might tell me. Julia, you have been a collaborator like no other. A million thanks to my editor, Tim Bartlett, to Alice Pfeifer, and to Laura Clark, not just for the excitement they shared for the book in its infancy, but for their support and patience with my very specific and stubborn vision once it came into being.

Finally, but before anyone else, there were the people who were my champions back when it felt daring to even show anyone my writing. I will never forget the kindness and generosity extended by Jody Rosen and Laurie Sandell—the first real writers to read my essays and tell me I could be one too. Without their thumbs-up I never would have had the courage to try. To Edie, who sat faithfully by my side for eleven years—I miss you terribly. And to my family—my grandmother, mother, father, and sister, all of whom are masterful storytellers in their own unique ways—thank you for loving me throughout every step of my own circuitous journey of exploration and discovery.

Index

Index

Index

Index

Index

Index

Index

Index

Index

Index

Index

Index

Index

Index

Index

Wiig, Kristin, 157, 158
wildness of language, 171, 173, 177.
    See also language
word choice. *See also* language
    audience and, 179–182
    authenticity and, 189–193
    Dee's speech, 190–191
    Sandra's speech, 187
    transitions and, 183–186
writing. *See also* speech writing
    author, writing background of,
        xxiii–xxvi
    book writing, 183–186

difficulty of, 192–193
"killing your darlings," 225
objectives for writing, 172

Y

Yagoda, Ben, 180
YouTube, xx

Z

zeitgeist, capturing the zeitgeist,
    29–38. *See also* influences of
    environment and the zeitgeist
Zoom, 31, 35–36